Charity Shops

Charity shops are now significant occupiers of the UK high street and are becoming familiar sites of consumption in the USA, Australia, Canada and Ireland. Acting as important fund-raisers for their parent charities, they work internationally, nationally and locally, linking the localities where they are situated with national or even global charitable endeavours, and chains of production and consumption. They also have a longer history than is, at first, apparent.

Charity Shops: retailing, consumption and society provides the first overview of the history, development and changing status of the charity shop. Material is drawn from a variety of disciplines, including marketing, retailing, cultural studies and social geography.

This book is based on widespread original research and current literature, offering an overview of the history and development of this retail phenomenon within a broader social, economic and environmental context. Particular reference is made to emerging alternative forms of retailing and lifestyles, gender issues, and flexible working practices. The authors draw on examples from the UK, Europe, Australia and North America.

With a wealth of new research, detailed discussion of context, and comparative perspectives, this book will be of special interest to all practitioners, researchers and students wishing to study the charity shop phenomenon.

Suzanne Horne is Senior Research Fellow in the Department of Marketing at the University of Stirling, with research interests primarily in the field of non-profit marketing. She has published widely on aspects of charity fund-raising with issues including affinity credit cards, charity shops and box collection schemes.

Avril Maddrell is Staff Tutor in Social Sciences at the Open University. In addition to her work on the history of geographical thought, Avril convened the first academic conference on charity shops in 1999, and co-edited the special issue of the *Journal of Nonprofit and Voluntary Sector Marketing* (2000) on charity shops with Suzanne Horne.

Routledge Studies in the Management of Voluntary and Non-Profit Organizations
Series Editor: Stephen P. Osborne

Charity Shops
Retailing, consumption and society

Suzanne Horne and Avril Maddrell

Taylor & Francis Group

LONDON AND NEW YORK

In memory of Gabriel

First published 2002 by Routledge
2 Park Square, Milton Park, Abingdon, Oxfordshire OX14 4RN

Simultaneously published in the USA and Canada
by Routledge
711 Third Avenue, New York, NY 10017

First issued in hardback 2014

Routledge is an imprint of the Taylor and Francis Group, an informa business

© 2002 Suzanne Horne and Avril Maddrell

Typeset in 10/12pt Sabon by Graphicraft Limited, Hong Kong

British Library Cataloguing in Publication Data
A catalogue record for this book is available from the
British Library

Library of Congress Cataloging in Publication Data
Horne, Suzanne.
    Charity shops: retailing, consumption and society/Suzanne
Horne and Avril Maddrell.
        p. cm.
    Includes bibliographical references and index.
    1. Thrift shops—Great Britain. I. Maddrell, Avril, 1964–
II. Title.

HF5482.4 .H67 2002
381′.19—dc21   2001058719

ISBN 13: 978-1-138-86398-9 (pbk)
ISBN 13: 978-0-415-25724-4 (hbk)

Contents

Illustrations

Acknowledgements

We are grateful to Henry Stewart Publications for permission to include material from Suzanne Horne's paper 'The charity shop: purpose and change', first published in the *International Journal of Nonprofit and Voluntary Sector Marketing*, vol. 5, no. 2, June 2000, pp. 113–24, Henry Stewart Publications, London, <www.henrystewart.com>.

We are grateful for the assistance of Joe Whiting, Fiona Allan and Nicole Krull at Taylor & Francis, as well as for the encouragement and input of series editor Stephen Osborne. We were also grateful for Peter Harrison's eagle-eyed copy-editing.

We would like to thank Sheila Sim at the Department of Marketing, University of Stirling, for her invaluable help with harmonising referencing, tables and layout in this volume.

We would also like to acknowledge the generous co-operation of charity shop managers, volunteers, shoppers and donors who have shared their experiences with us, as well as the patience and support of our colleagues and families throughout the writing process. Ultimately, we would like to acknowledge each other, as neither of us would have written the book without the other.

Note on the text

To provide anonymity for specific charity shops, managers, volunteers etc., each shop in the Oxford, Isle of Man and Liverpool samples were given a letter for identification purposes. Similarly, where there were multiple responses such as volunteers or donors, each was given a number in addition to their shop code. The same letter is used for all those associated with a given shop e.g. Manager B, Oxford, Volunteer 9, Oxford B. This allows the reader to identify where information is drawn from the same and different sources. It also allows cross referencing of sources within and between chapters.

Introduction

Charity shops are now significant occupiers of the UK high street and are becoming familiar sights and sites of consumption in the USA, Australia, Canada and Ireland. They act as important fund-raisers for their parent charities, working internationally, nationally or locally, linking the localities where they are situated with national or even global charitable endeavours and chains of production and consumption. In common with many 'phenomena', charity shops have a longer history than is first apparent; this history and the growth of the sector in the UK is mapped out in brief below, to provide a context for the contemporary charity retailing sector.

The origins of charity retailing can be traced at least as far back as the latter part of the nineteenth century. In 1890 William Booth, founder of the Salvation Army, wrote *In Darkest England and the Way Out*, reviewing what was perceived as the crisis of the social conditions of the working classes of the time. He discussed what was needed to 'elevate the submerged' in society at that time, suggesting that there was a large amount of wastage of goods in well-to-do homes which could be channelled into supplying the 'submerged' with employment. This employment would manifest itself in the collection of quality second-hand goods from these affluent homes and would also be channelled into the renovation of less perfect goods in order to make them serviceable for further use. He organised teams of men to collect from these well-to-do Victorian homes and was at great pains to make sure that he was not taking goods away from other charities or charitable causes of the time. The goods collected were then sold from 'salvage stores' in London and provincial centres (Horne 2000).

Plate 0.1 is taken from the Salvation Army publication *The War Cry* of 8 February 1908 and shows the salvage store in Leeds. The original caption for the picture was 'By means of this store wastage from the homes of the wealthy is turned to profitable account in the

Plate 0.1 The Salvage Store, Leeds – where second-hand clothing, furniture, etc. could be had very cheaply

Source: The Salvation Army International Heritage Centre. Reproduced with permission

service of the poor and submerged.' The store was in a building attached to the 'Men's Metropole' in Lisbon Street, Leeds, and was open for business twice a week operating under the joint management of Adjutant and Mrs Sansom. The merchandise mix of the store was extremely diverse. The content was listed as follows:

> Vast assortment of miscellaneous headgear for men; collars, fronts and white shirts offered at remarkable prices.
> Heaps of umbrellas – most needing repair; ladies' millinery; rolls of used linoleum; skirts, mantles, blouses, underwear, boots and shoes, dancing pumps and wellington boots.

All reasonably predictable, but the list goes on: 'sponge and hip baths, a crippled sewing machine, a meat chopper, a mangle roller, perambulators, mail-carts and bassinets. Also included is glass and china ware, furniture both large and small and even two useless firearms!' The goods were apparently arranged 'to good advantage' and every article was priced 'so as to avoid haggling and beating down' by customers. The description by the shop manager of one customer purchasing a cart, only to return it later claiming a broken wheel-spoke, is reminiscent of interviews with late twentieth-century charity shop managers recorded in Chapter 3.

After the original store in London, other stores were opened throughout England, the USA and Canada before 1914, thus realising the internationalisation of the charity shop early in the twentieth century. A report from the store in New York (Sandall 1955) suggests that at first customers there were interested in 'striking a bargain' and purchasing goods that they needed at a low price. However, after the initial contact for goods they were offered a spiritual contact and a new insight into a better way of life. William Booth's main aim was to ease the living conditions of the poor and at the same time proclaim the Gospel of Christ to all who came into the shops.

In addition to selling through the salvage stores, a salvage centre warehouse was established at Battersea Wharf in London. This was a concept far ahead of its time, but was interrupted by the advent of the First World War. The idea is now being seen as a way forward for distribution methods for modern charity shops (see Chapter 4). The original salvage centre was opened in response to the vast amounts of goods collected by General Booth's collectors. So much newspaper and cloth was collected that a warehouse was needed to store the goods until their disposal (*The Social Gazette*, 1896). This distribution centre flourished at Battersea, giving work to the unemployed and providing exports to continental Europe and North America. Its operation was brought to a virtual halt at the outbreak of the First World War, and distribution centres on this scale were not seen again until the end of the century.

After the advances of Victorian charity retail and distribution, the charity shop concept was fairly dormant in the UK throughout the period of the First and Second World Wars, but was more widespread in the USA in the inter-war years of economic depression. This period, as regards the charity shop concept, was characterised by Mary McCarthy (1954: 278–9) in *The Group*, when Polly's father, Mr Andrews, finds employment as a paid assistant in a thrift shop, demonstrating both the character of the goods on offer and social attitudes attached to the exchange of second-hand goods:

> 'The stuff is all donated. . . . We have second-hand furs, children's clothes, old dinner jackets, maids' and butlers' uniforms. A great many of those thanks to the late unpleasantness.' This was her father's name for the depression. Polly frowned; she did not like the

thought of her father selling old clothes. 'They come from the best houses,' he said. 'And there are amusing French dolls and music boxes. Armoires, etageres, jardinières. Whatnots, umbrella stands, marble topped commodes. Gilt chairs for musicales. Gold headed canes, fawn gloves, opera hats, fans, Spanish combs and mantillas, a harp. Horsehair sofas. An instructive inventory of the passé.'

The charity shop as we know it in the UK today is a post-1945 phenomenon. In 1947 Oxfam opened its first shop, which was the first modern charity shop. The Oxfam committee had appealed to the public for clothes and blankets for Greek women and children who were suffering because of the uprising in Greece in 1946. The response to its appeal was so positive that there was a surplus of goods that had to be disposed of in a useful way and it was decided to convert these goods into cash in order to raise funds for their continuing work. The result of this conversion of goods into cash resulted in the birth of the world's largest charity retailing business. The original shop is still in operation in Broad Street in Oxford (Plate 0.2).

Plate 0.2 The original Oxfam shop, Broad Street, Oxford, in 2001 – offering second-hand and new goods, fair trade products and photocopying services (Photograph: A. Maddrell)

The Sue Ryder Foundation followed Oxfam's lead when in the early 1950s it opened shops in London, Birmingham, Hull, Manchester and Liverpool (Horne 2000). However, it was not until the 1960s that the growth phase really began. In the 1960s incomes were increasing and society was moving into the era of consumer disposables. The culture was one of buy and discard rather than the wartime ethos of make do and mend. Goods, especially clothes, that were too good to throw away were donated to the charities for them to convert into cash donations. The most widespread form of selling was the jumble sale, commonly supporting local causes and interests or local branches of nation-wide organisations such as the Scout and Guide movements, churches or political parties. Formal shops often developed through the realisation of the potential of clothing sales, and for the most part these first shops were run by volunteers for a few hours a day and were located in secondary or poor locations, close to the people who needed the goods that were on sale. During the next twenty years many charities opened shops, often in temporary sites, but the most rapid expansion in their development has taken place since 1985, at which time the economy of the United Kingdom was on an upturn and there was greater disposable wealth and surplus goods were in abundance.

However, while there was a buoyant economy this was far from uniform, and the Conservative government's policy in the 1980s was to cut social services, making it necessary for charities to carry out more work in society, for example in mental health provision, housing and home care. This in turn resulted in an ever-increasing need for charities to raise unallocated money – that is, an income stream that was available for use and not tied to any specific project. The shrinking government funding was coupled with a decline in pure donations due to the recession in the late 1980s, and consequently charities were faced with rising costs, and more competition for fewer donations and grants. As a consequence, non-profit organisations turned even more to the for-profit world to leverage their traditional sources of funding. Non-profit leaders viewed earned-income-generated activities as more reliable funding sources than donations and grants (Dees 1998), and in the charity sector, charity retailing proved to be one of the most popular trading activities for raising money.

It is difficult to give accurate figures for numbers of charity shops emerging in the 1980s because there is little documentation and the sector was both very diverse and dynamic. However, the expansion in shop numbers can be clearly seen in the case of a specific charity such as the Sue Ryder Foundation. As can be seen from Table 0.1, this

Table 0.1 Number of Sue Ryder shops in operation from 1982 to 1992

Year	SR
1982	126
1983	134
1984	153
1985	187
1986	243
1987	275
1988	340
1989	364
1990	394
1991	464
1992	451

Source: After Horne and Broadbridge (1995)

Table 0.2 Number of charity shops, 1990–8

Year	No. of shops
1990	2,852
1991	3,097
1992	3,476
1993	3,738
1994	4,009
1995	4,199
1996	4,454
1997	6,238
1998	5,771

Source: After Phelan (1999)

Note: The numbers in this table give the total number of shops belonging to the fifty-three charities described by Phelan (1999)

charity opened 325 shops in the eleven-year period 1982–92. From the beginning of the 1990s there was a steady increase in the number of charities opening shops and the expansion of existing chains, with Oxfam operating the largest chain with 873 shops followed by the Sue Ryder Foundation with 585 in 1997.

However, the sector did not experience simple linear growth in the number of shops and it is estimated that of the 5,223 shops in operation in 1998, 170 were closed down and a further 427 opened (Phelan *et al.* 1998). This movement of shop numbers resulted in a net gain of 257 shops, which is just under 5 per cent. The large charity chains opened the most new shops but also closed the most. The

British Red Cross increased its shop numbers by 12 but closed 28 shops in 1998 and Oxfam closed 27 shops and opened 36 more. Of the 39 main charity retailers, 25 expected to increase the number of their shops while 10 expected to keep the same number, resulting in the expectation that the overall number of shops would increase by 5 per cent a year (Phelan *et al.* 1998). See Table 0.2, which is based on information on 53 charities and represents an increase of 102 per cent in nine years; and Table 0.3, which illustrates the growth in the number of shops opened by individual charities.

This steady increase in growth indicates that the value of the retail sector to the financial viability of the charity sector was truly recognised. The more income derived from the shops, the more dependent the charities became on them and the more effort was devoted to them and infrastructure developed.

With in excess of 6,000 retail outlets and a turnover of approximately £350 million (Goodall 2000c), charity shops have become significant players both on the high street and within the broader voluntary sector. Growth in numbers of shops since the 1980s has been accompanied by a number of changes, notably in retail presentation and practice and in increased competition for volunteers and donors (Horne and Maddrell 2000). What has been described as the 'professionalisation' of the sector, achieved mainly through the increased employment of paid staff (especially managers) at shop level and the introduction of mainstream retailing methods in charity shops, has resulted in a number of tensions within charity shops and between these and competitive mainstream retailers (see Chapter 2). However, this 'professionalisation' of charity shops has been far from universal or uniform, and the sector is now recognised as incorporating a continuum of operational types which encompasses such variety that it disrupts the notion of a homogeneous 'sector' at all (Horne and Maddrell 2000). Outlet growth has resulted in competition between the growing number of charity shops for volunteers – exceeded only by competition for donated goods (see Chapter 4) – as shops continue to rely heavily on an estimated workforce of 100,000 largely female volunteer staff. This has resulted in innovative partnerships between individual charity shops and different cohorts of locally accessible volunteers (Maddrell 2000). Notably these have included those needing some form of rehabilitation into, or reparation to, society with many of these partnerships being 'indicative of complex interrelationships between individual charity shops and broader community, both state and civil society' (Horne and Maddrell 2000: 102; and see Chapter 5).

Table 0.3 Growth in the number of charity shops, 1990–8

Year	Oxfam	Imperial Cancer Research Fund (ICRF)	Age Concern England	British Red Cross	Help the Aged	Barnardo's	SCOPE	British Heart Foundation	Cancer Research Campaign	Save the Children
1990	804	400	150	152	114	273	185	13	150	128
1991	821	425	160	141	142	278	204	70	150	146
1992	843	468	200	190	185	291	238	111	190	153
1993	836	470	237	285	213	294	246	147	190	160
1994	842	470	327	306	240	307	250	192	207	159
1995	842	470	367	324	280	307	254	225	227	158
1996	844	474	400	355	322	315	276	272	234	158
1997	873	468	400	425	362	332	302	350	255	154
1998	847[a]	465	406	448	380	323	314	383	267	154

Source: Adapted from Phelan (1999)

Note:
a Excluding Ireland

The growth of the charity shop sector has generated competition with 'commercial retailers', with small business owners expressing opposition to charity shops in local chambers of commerce and media. This opposition has had wider ramifications, resulting in the UK government's review of the taxation status of charity trading. The real and perceived elements of this trading conflict are an issue that again has grown with the professionalisation of the charity shop sector. However, these concerns vary between areas, reflecting both individual relationships between the staff of a given charity shop and local retailers, the number of charity shops in a locality and the economic well-being of an area (see Chapters 2 and 7).

In charity shopping we meet a particular form of the universal juxtaposition and integration of material goods and values shaped by the socio-economic-political-cultural lens of individuals and societies that comes into play in all forms of consumption. The emerging purchasing patterns associated with charity shops suggest a number of different purchasing strategies used by different types of shopper, with customers seeking to minimise expenditure, or enhance purchasing power, variety or collectability (see Chapter 3 on customers and Chapter 6 on price and competition). There appears to be increasing openness to second-hand goods in general in the UK, with recycling, fair trade and retro fashion all representing variables in consumer decision-making, with charity shops having played a significant role in 'normalising the purchase of second hand everyday goods' (Horne and Maddrell 2000: 102).

In attempting an overview of the charity shop, we have drawn on a number of approaches, particularly our own respective disciplinary backgrounds of retailing and marketing and social and cultural geography. In merging these approaches in a consideration of charity shops, inevitably tensions sometimes arise and some readers may be predisposed to one element over the other. However, while there is the possibility of taking different routes through the book, we would argue that these tensions merely reflect those found within the charity shop sector itself, spanning as it does retailing and consumption, volunteering and paid work, local and (inter)national networks.

These tensions can be seen in the questions considered in subsequent chapters, which are central to understanding the charity shop. Are charity shops a marketing or a social phenomenon? Are customers driven by economic, social, political or cultural motives? Is voluntary labour gradually being undermined by paid staff? Should charity shops maximise profits for their charity or provide cheap goods to the needy? Are charity shops being used by the needy? Are charity shops merely another retail-offering niche or do they have wider implications for society? Do any of these apparent oppositions have to be mutually exclusive? In charity shops we see a blending of processes and experiences that combine all of the above and we have tried to reflect this in our consideration of retailing, consumption, working and socialising through the use, space or locale of the charity shop.

The topography of charity shops in all senses constitutes a shifting landscape, with individual charities simultaneously opening and closing shops within their local, regional, national or even international networks, while other charities commence trading for the first time and others cease trading in the face of falling income. Rather than trying to hit a moving target, we have given a series of snapshots of the changing sector and have focused on drawing out trends and issues discernible from individual place-specific research studies such as Maddrell on Oxford, Liverpool and the Isle of Man, Horne and Broadridge's Scottish work, as well as longitudinal sector-wide studies such as the annual Non-governmental Organisation (NGO) Finance Survey, which maps the contours of (known/provided) shop and volunteer numbers, turnover and profit levels.

In blending material from marketing, retailing, cultural studies and social geography, we are conscious that readers from different backgrounds may be inclined to different routes through this book. For example, charity retailers might be more interested in Chapter 2 on retail theory than in Chapter 1 with its focus on consumption and identity. Whatever route is taken, it is hoped that the contents of this book will prove useful to both researchers and practitioners alike.

1 Consumption, identity and locality

A theoretical perspective on charity shops I

Placing the charity shop in its theoretical context is a complex task, reflecting the character of the sector itself. Each of the differing aspects of charity retailing, volunteerism and the consumption of primarily second-hand goods (with its reference to socio-economic status, lifestyle and identity) needs to be considered. Place is also a significant part of context that needs to be recognised here, in terms of (a) the general UK context of most of the book, (b) similarities and contrasts with charity and thrift shops in other countries, and (c) the specificities of local contexts. Hence it is necessary to mesh together a number of theoretical perspectives in order to begin to situate charity shops. However, inevitably, this will represent a starting place for more specific theoretical contexts relating to engagements with particular facets of charity shops' operations, functions, and spatial and social relations, for as Mort (1996) notes, consumption studies have often been guilty of over-abstraction and generalisation.

Recent publications have placed retail studies within the theoretical framework of the political economy or sociological studies of culture, notably the edited collections of Miller (1995a), Wrigley and Lowe (1996) and Jackson et al. (2000). These have marked a change from retail- to consumption-led research, with the emphasis being on 'consumption as a dynamic socially constructed activity' (Wrigley and Lowe 1996: 19). Within these studies, geographies of consumption have tended to focus on three areas: the changing sites of consumption; the chains that link consumption's multiple locations; and spaces and places of contemporary consumption (Jackson and Thrift 1995), although it has been noted that sites, spaces and places are often indistinguishable (Wrigley and Lowe 1996).

As sites of both spaces *and* places of consumption, the formal retailing sector, and above all the department store and the mall, have dominated this work. However, the whole area of 'alternative' retailing is emerging as a fertile one for study, particularly given the links between changing socio-economic and spatial relations in, for example, home shopping, peripatetic markets, jumble sales, car boot sales as well as charity shops. The recent increase in the theoretical and empirical engagement with issues relating to alternative retailing and consumption, for example second-hand children's clothes, Tupperware parties (Clarke 1998, 2000), car boot sales (Gregson and Crewe 1997a, b, 1998) and the Internet (Slater 2000), is evidence of this trend.

The charity shop sector, retailing primarily second-hand goods, burgeoned in the UK in the 1980s and 1990s, growing to 6,000 shops nation-wide, with a turnover of £350 million and drawing on 100,000 volunteers (Phelan 1998). There has also been significant growth in the sector in Australia, where they are known as Opportunity or 'Opp' shops, and a steady increase in the USA, where they are known as (not-for-profit) thrift shops. The rapid growth in numbers of charity shops in the UK began to tail off in the late 1990s with the apparent saturation of the market (see Chapter 2). Somewhat ironically, this apparent peaking and relative stagnation of the charity retail sector at the *fin de siècle* has coincided with an increase in the theoretical and empirical engagement with the neglected field of alternative retailing and consumption. Arguably a retailing phenomenon in the 1980s and 1990s, charity shops are characterised by their complex relationships between charity and retailing, shop and locality, consumption and re-cycling, volunteers and paid staff (especially professional managers). In turn, these complex relationships represent a wealth of insight into consumption choices and related socio-economic and lifestyle groups, volunteering culture and the changing role of civil society within local and national contexts.

Consumption, lifestyle and locality

In order to understand the charity shop as a potential site of 'alternative' consumption, it is necessary to consider the character of contemporary consumption culture and practices. Consumption culture is a characteristic of broader material culture (person–thing relations) which emerged in Euro-American industrialised societies in the second half of the twentieth century (Lury 1999). While the literal definition of consumption implies the using up of a thing, the word is more accurately denoted simply as 'using'. This is particularly significant to the study of second-hand goods as it allows a move away from looking at consumption as a singular linear process from production to market and consumption, accommodating alternative systems of exchange or cycles of production or consumption that are particularly pertinent to charity shops, notably extended and complex cycles of consumption (Miller 1998; Lury 1999) – cycles that encompass successive chains (Gregson *et al.* 2000). Acknowledging these multiple cycles of consumption raises questions about the life history of material goods, and Kopytoff (1986) has asked a number of questions particularly relevant to the study of second-hand goods: Where do goods come from? What has been their career so far? What is considered an ideal career for a given item? How does an object's use and status change? What happens when it is at the end of its useful life? Appadurai's (1986) notion of animating or giving 'social lives' to objects (see Lury 1999) is also particularly helpful when considering these cycles and questions, as this approach focuses on the changing status of goods over time and the ways in which these goods produce social identity, which in turn is linked to lifestyle.

Engagement with consumption practices had been rather sidelined by the modernist separation of economics and culture (Shields 1992); however, within the context of seemingly exponential growth of consumer demand, both commercial and academic commentators in the UK identified the 1980s as significant in the transition from production- to consumption-led values. This switch was identified as being founded on the 'appearance of intensified forms of individualism', with (increased) consumption being founded on self-reflexivity (the cultivation of self) (Mort 1996). However, it is important in looking at contemporary consumption that the mistake is not made of disengaging economics from our understanding of consumption, which is inherently based upon economic exchange: economics and culture are both enmeshed and mutually constituted (Blomley 1996). However, while increased consumption might suggest universally increased access to goods, this is not necessarily the case. This can be seen nowhere more clearly than in the case of poverty (often compounded by gender and racial differences), with a significant proportion of people in Euro-American societies living in poverty, limiting their participation in consumer culture. This constitutes a significant issue in relation to the socio-economic functions of charity shops (along with other forms of low-cost consumption) in the consumption practices of the economically disadvantaged. To what extent do low-cost sites of consumption afford opportunities for agency and enfranchisement in consumer culture? Or is it that the necessity of using these shops is merely a reflection of the constraints of economic structures? Alternatively, is the consumption of second-hand goods in the charity shop rejected by the poor as symbolic of economic failure? Or, moreover, are the prices of second-hand goods in some charity shops beyond the purchasing power of the poorest in society?

Mintel (1997) suggests that twice as many people from socio-economic class E (30 per cent) use charity shops in the UK than people from classes A and B (15 per cent). However, this is not a simple correlation, as the relatively high rate of use of charity shops by the highest social classes is still significant – as Miller (1998) suggests, thrift is a near-universal motivation. As Lury (1999) notes, the relationship between relative wealth and participation in material culture is both very complex and historically variable (as is borne out in Chapter 3, which looks at shoppers' motivations and consumption practices). Moreover, consumption strategies used in charity shops also raise questions concerning the 'alternative' character of this form of consumption. Do charity shops represent opportunities to resist the discourses and power relations of mainstream retailing, or, as Gregson and Rose (2000) suggest in the case of car boot sales, an opportunity for many to avail themselves of this discourse in their lives more cheaply, for example through access to second-hand status labels or brands?

Consumption is influenced by a number of factors – a desire to emulate status, hedonism, escapism, fantasy, novelty or 'identity value' (Lury 1999) – but analysis of consumption has tended to focus on the consumption of cultural goods, to the neglect of more functional shopping. This has been addressed in part by Miller (1998), who looks at household provisioning and maintenance in north London. Charity shops similarly cut across the functional/cultural dualism, and the aim in this volume is to place charity shops and people's engagement with them – including consumption – within the complex cultural, socio-economic and local contexts, while at the same time allowing general observations to be made. Consumption encompasses price and economic relations, as well as the cultural element, including meaning and value. Goods are consumed not only in order to fulfil functional needs, but to act as meaningful markers of social relations, and thereby become visible and stable signs by which we classify people in society – commodities become 'recognisable signposts in the process of self-enactment demanded by society' (Mort 1996: 11). Goods become endowed with meaning which (although subject to change) can represent personal qualities, interests and interpersonal influence, and become part of a system of symbolic exchange (Douglas and Isherwood 1979 cited by Lury 1999). This symbolism can be seen in the case of manufactured goods signifying membership of a wider group, paralleling in anthropological terms a form of totemism whereby an object represents both natural and cultural elements and is symbolic of a greater whole (Sahlins 1976 cited by Lury 1999). These social groups identified by their particular 'symbols' and signifiers have been described as 'tribes' and can be seen most vividly in terms of clothing, which represents specific lifestyle choices. These tribes notably include bikers, punks and New Age travellers, but office workers also are a 'tribe' (see McDowell 1996 on dress codes and gender in the City financial sector in London), as are the middle classes generally. While modern forms of solidarity and communality based on class, gender, occupation and locality have been undermined by individualisation (Beck 1992 cited by Mort 1996), different groupings have been formed through loose sociation, resulting in unstable non-ascriptive 'neo-tribes' that may share beliefs and lifestyle – consumption playing a significant role in maintaining group identity (Hetherington 1992).

Thus consumption can be seen as a type of social exchange: 'consumption both solidifies the sense of the personal self, and confirms it as social through common membership in a shopping fraternity' (Shields 1992: 15). Consumption, particularly of cultural goods, can also act to create oppositional identities or concretise a group identity – for example, the positive process of reinforcing a marginalised racial identity through consumption practices (i.e. part of Hall's (1992) self-construction, cited by Lury (1999)). This notion of sociality-based *bündes* mediates between Tönnies's (1887) dualism of *gessellschaft* and *gemeinschaft*, representing a trans-modern form of association, providing a collective sense of belonging and normality in an affirmative but unstable grouping, rather than the 'contract' community of *gemeinschaft* (Shields 1992). While the concept of affectual neo-tribes or *bündes* might apply to types of shoppers, or even volunteers in charity shops (see Chapter 5 on volunteers), Shields suggests that particular forms of consumption engender, if not community as such, then a looser form of sociality in relation to the interaction of people, place and consumption culture. This is a theme that will be explored in Chapters 3, 5 and 7 with regard to the relationship between charity shops and their locality, given their dependence on largely local volunteer labour, consumers and donors – that is, the production, marketing and consumption of the charity shop offering.

If symbolic meanings are central to understanding consumption practices in general, then it is necessary that this debate be placed within the context of retailing and consumption within the charity shop sector, particularly in relation to the symbolic meaning of different types of second-hand goods. The symbolic meanings attributed to goods are subject to change, and according to Kopytoff this movability and transformability of meaning is a result of long-term and large-scale socio-economic and political relations, and the often linked life history or 'cultural biography' of an object as it changes hands, contexts, etc. (see Kopytoff 1986 cited by Lury 1999).

However, the more micro-elements of short-term fashion and changing personal circumstances are not to be underestimated in this equation. It is these varied changes that often render goods surplus to requirements, transforming the once desired object to something unwanted; what might once have been considered inalienable becomes alienable, disposable, and so objects are dispatched on their next 'journey' within the extended cycle of consumption. This for many reusable goods in contemporary British society means being consigned to the charity shop or car boot sale, or in American society the thrift shop or garage sale, rather than the proverbial 'junk heap'. Indeed, the sale of second-hand goods depends upon their alienable status to the previous owners, but this does not preclude them from becoming inalienable goods to another consumer, especially if something is deemed collectable. While 'the meaning of goods can be transferred, obscured or confused, or even lost when goods change hands', emphasising the mutability of meaning, these processes are often mediated by fear – fear of loss of identity on the part of the relinquisher and fear of the previous owner's identity in the case of the acquisitor (Lury 1999). The latter can be seen explicitly in the case of second-hand clothing (see Chapter 3 and Gregson *et al.* 2000), where the *psychological* ritual of cleansing can be as important as the actual *physical* process of cleaning used clothing, either as divesting one's own association with an item before giving it away or, more commonly, divesting the associations of another/an 'other' (see McCracken 1988).

Second and subsequent cycles of consumption

> What amazed me was the sheer volume of objects, remnants of lives, and the way they circulated. The people died but their possessions did not, they went around and around as in a slow eddy. All of the things I saw and coveted had been seen and coveted previously, they had passed through several lives and were destined to pass through several more, becoming more worn but also more valuable, harder and more brilliant, as if they had absorbed their owner's sufferings and fed on them. How difficult these objects are to dispose of, I thought; they lurk passively, like vampire sheep, waiting for someone to buy them.
>
> (Margaret Atwood (1982), *Lady Oracle*)

Different attitudes to second-hand goods can be embedded in different socio-economic class, ethnic or national cultures. For example, Oxfam experienced resistance to buying second-hand clothes when it set up shops in Germany, and there is widespread distaste for second-hand goods in Japan, where even the market for used books is small (see Clammer 1992). The culture of multiple cycles of consumption via formal systems of exchange seems to be best established in former British settler colonies, such as the USA and Australia. Formal institutions often played a role in this process, such as political parties and churches. For example, the Catholic charity St Vincent de Paul run chains of charity shops in Ireland, USA, Canada and Australia, raising money to support largely local social programmes such as the provision of soup kitchens and other support for the homeless. In Australia, where the discourse of environmental stewardship and recycling goods is well developed in some areas and some social groups, charity shops run alongside second-hand shops, including good-as-new, which often adopt an environmental tag for marketing their goods, e.g. 'Recycle Rags'. Other markets are emerging for recycled goods, such as the former Soviet bloc, where 'Western' clothes are desired as symbols of identity (see Rausing 1998). Such markets involve the international transfer of second-hand goods, whether as gifts or as commercial enterprise, but this is not new.

Consumption is riddled with different (cultural) ritual processes, notably in relation to possession (collecting, displaying, cleaning), gifting (such as for birthdays) and divestment (for example, erasing a meaning in order to give something away) (McCracken 1988), all of which are relevant to the particular chain of consumption experienced through charity shops, as well as other consumption sites. Miller (1998) refines this idea of ritual in his *Theory of Shopping*, based on the shopping practices of people living in a north London street, suggesting that love and devotion are at the heart of day-to-day shopping (especially provisioning) – that, in contrast to popular perceptions and media images, rather than being self-centred hedonism, shopping has a parallel with ritual sacrifice in serving others, real or imagined. This idea is grounded in the secularisation of industrialised Western society, whereby romantic and familial love has become a substitute for religious devotion, giving commodities the status of the material culture of love, particularly as expressed by women to their loved ones. Women make 80 per cent of purchasing decisions in the UK (Miller 1998), and housework (including shopping) was widely recognised in the second half of the twentieth century as representing an 'ideal' expression of love and warmth (Lury 1999). Commodities are used to 'constitute the complexity of contemporary social relations' (Miller 1998: 8), with the ultimate goal (as with ritual sacrifice) of creating a desiring subject through the devotional act of shopping, but also with the concomitant object of implicitly or explicitly attempting to influence the recipient into becoming the type of person for whom the commodity is appropriate (for example, an interview suit for an unemployed youth). However, as Marx noted in his argument about the fetishism of commodities (and Miller recognises in respect of some people not in partnerships), not only do commodities shroud the social relations of production, but they can also stand in for relations between people (Lury 1999).

In the first instance it might appear difficult to create both a desiring and an enhanced subject as the result of the purchase of second-hand items from charity shops, given the association with soiled cast-offs. However, there is some purchase in relation to the opportunity for the 'upgrading' of consumption opportunities (see Gregson and Crewe 1998), as well as the second-hand selling point of the opportunity to acquire authentic retro goods, often crucial to collectors or particular lifestyle groups or 'tribes'. The majority of shopping constitutes a form of domestic servicing: goods necessary for the reproduction of labour and families. However, Miller argues that every-day consumption choices demonstrate 'how shoppers develop and imagine those social relationships which they care about through the medium of selecting goods' (1998: 5), thereby elevating shopping from functional to social experience. These everyday goods are contrasted with the 'treat', and for many shoppers are grounded in some notion of thrift (Miller 1998) (see Chapter 3). This concept of thrift is central to understanding the motivations of many of the shoppers in charity shops, as witnessed by the fact that outlets in the second-hand market, including not-for-profit charity shops, are known as *thrift* shops in North America. Miller (1998) has suggested that 'experiencing shopping as saving money' is a central ritual aspect of consumption regardless of socio-economic status. Indeed, he suggests that thrift is a transcendent life goal. Certainly the hunt for a bargain underpins much of charity shop consumption.

Part of the thesis of this book relates to the actual or potential role that charity shops can perform within their localities. Social theory in the past has tended to focus on large formal institutions or individuals, missing out the middle ground, especially local organisations (Milofsky 1988a). However, postmodernism has encouraged the examination of social phenomena within their specific context. The notion of 'community' (rather like national identity) is primarily a mental construct, as well as being a background factor in most people's lives, which means that there has been relatively little research on how community organisations work, or how they function as an independent variable within society (ibid.). Despite this, Milofsky (ibid.) argues that community and neighbourhood organisations are a primary vehicle of change in local areas. We are not suggesting here that charity shops are necessarily community organisations – indeed, in the majority of cases, the contrary is the case. However, we do suggest that charity shops fulfil a number of functions that can contribute to the creation of social networks within the locale of the shop and the wider locality (see Chapters 5 and 7). A charity shop constitutes a particular locale or use space, a physical setting that is socially defined. For example, the physical space of a charity shop might be very similar to that of a neighbouring shop, but its social structures and patterns of social relationships might be quite different.

Giddens used the notion of the locale as a means of explaining the interaction of people and social structures, seeing social structures as both the *means* and the *product* of human interaction (Dickens 1990). The idea of locale can be applied to the use space of the charity shop as a whole, as well as the demarcation of space (and occupations) within the shop, notably 'front' and 'back' shop space, with the latter associated with the unseen 'private' work of cleansing and sorting (see Chapter 5 on volunteer attitudes to 'front' and 'back' work, also Gregson *et al.* 2000). Networks of association are created within the locale of the charity shop by dint of its social structures, and those structures in turn can be influenced by those networks – depending upon the reflexivity of the management structure within the organisation (see Goodall 2000c).

However, Dickens (1990: 3) argues that we should also recognise the locality, in the sense of a 'local social system', in addition to the particular use space of the locale, incorporating an expressive and biotic order that accommodates people's instinctive interactions with one another and their environment, cutting across a dualistic sense of structure and agency. This sense of locality is particularly important in the face of 'ontological uncertainty' in a world of stretched social relations (see Dickens 1990 on Giddens). Just as consumption can be a means of expressing individual and collective identity, civil society – including voluntary organisations such as charity shops – can afford an opportunity for individual agency in constructing identity and a sense of belonging within a locality. Within the locale of the charity shop (itself within the wider context of the locality), these different opportunities for identity construction can coincide, being especially embodied in volunteers and regular customers with a strong commitment to the ethos of the particular charity and/or its trading practices.

2 Retailing

A theoretical perspective on charity shops II

The historic roots of the charity shop, as described in the Introduction, show that the underlying philosophy of the sector is grounded in social service. However, since those early days the sector has developed and changed in character, encompassing diversity of approach to the business of charity retailing. This diversity has implications for our understanding of the ethos, retailing practices, management systems and customer base of charity shops, individually and collectively.

Classification of charity shops

Characterisation of charity shops as if they formed a homogenous group is increasingly a misrepresentation of the sector. In the early 1980s shops were more uniform in nature but, as the sector has developed, there has been polarisation in terms of store size, store function, the merchandise mix and the development of chains of stores, as opposed to the autonomous unit. An attempt has been made to classify stores (Horne and Broadbridge 1995) on the basis of merchandise mix. They suggest that depending on the type of merchandise sold, it is possible to classify charity shops into the following three categories:

Category I	100 per cent donated merchandise
Category II	Donated merchandise plus a proportion of new merchandise
Category III	100 per cent new merchandise.

Category I comprises those charity shops that sell only donated second-hand goods, ranging from clothes and furniture to books and smaller household items. In these shops most second-hand goods donated to the shops are accepted and offered for sale, the exception being those goods restricted by law, usually because of a safety aspect, for example

Table 2.1 Category II merchandise mix

Percentage of retail outlets	Percentage donated goods	Percentage bought-in goods
48	95	5
24	90	10
4	85	15
4	75	25
8	70	30
4	65	35
4	50	50
4	5	95

Source: Authors' research and Corporate Intelligence (1992)

firearms or drugs, and safety wear such as child car seats and buoyancy devices. Electrical goods can be accepted for sale but have to be tested by a qualified person using appropriate testing equipment. Some charities do not accept large white goods because, although they can be tested electrically and found to be working, the quality of performance cannot be tested. Second-hand toys can be sold but have to conform to the same safety standard as new toys – that is, British Standard BS EN71 (BS 5655). Moreover, some charities refuse to sell second-hand shoes and earrings for pierced ears, for health reasons. The law on furnishing fabrics implemented in 1988 restricts the sale of any covered seating to that manufactured after 1988 which carries a fireproof label, and the sale of other furniture is restricted because of the difficulties of transporting, handling and storing it. Any goods deemed unfit for resale are usually accepted but thrown away or recycled via an alternative route – for example, ragging, whereby clothes unfit for sale are sold on for recycling in other forms such as car seat upholstery (see Chapter 4).

Category II comprises shops that, in addition to selling donated goods, sell a percentage of new bought-in goods, with a merchandise mix of between 5 per cent and 95 per cent of bought-in goods (Table 2.1). As charities have grown in retail professionalism, so they have changed the nature of their retail operations. One of the major changes has been the buying-in of new merchandise, a change that occurred during the second half of the 1980s and coincided with the rapid expansion of charity shops in the UK at that time. The rationale for the changed strategy was, first, to improve the image of the shops in order to attract new customers and thus widen the customer base, and second, to compensate for the lack of good-quality goods being donated to the shops (Horne 1998). In the late 1980s many people were feeling the effect of the recession and were not renewing their clothes and household goods to the same extent. The amount of good-quality goods being donated to the charity shops was in decline, and without a constant provision of donated goods the shops could not exist, or at best could not be as profitable. Many people, instead of donating to charity shops, were selling their disposable goods at car boot sales for their own enjoyment and financial reward (Stone *et al.* 1996; see also Crewe and Gregson 1998; Gregson and Crewe, 1998).

The new goods that are bought-in for sale in charity shops include craft-type goods (often from industrialising countries), stationery, pottery, jewellery and household goods. The bought-in goods tend to be relatively low-cost 'gift' items. They are often displayed in the windows so as to attract potential customers into the shop. Inside the shop the new goods are generally displayed separately from the donated goods, in a clear demarcation of use and consumer identity space.

From Table 2.1 it can be seen that the percentage of bought-in goods is variable, and Horne and Broadbridge (1995) suggest that because of this, Category II can be further subdivided into Category IIa (donated second-hand goods and up to 35 per cent bought-in new goods) and Category IIb (donated second-hand goods and more than 35 per cent bought-in new goods). This subdivision categorises, respectively, those shops that sell mainly donated goods and are therefore 'charity shops' and those that enter the seemingly more 'commercial' arena.

The reason for this watershed between converted donation and retail commercialism is the tax implications that surround the charity shop. Value added tax (VAT) is charged on bought-in goods but is not charged on goods donated by the public to the charity shops. The business rate charged for trading in a location varies according to the location, but the local authority in which the shop operates has to give an 80 per cent business rate relief to a charity shop. This relief can be further reduced as the authorities are able to add a further discretionary 20 per cent discount. Thus a charging authority gives a mandatory rates relief of 80 per cent and a discretionary relief of 20 per cent. It is suggested that in order to qualify for relief of these taxes, the turnover of bought-in goods must not exceed 35 per cent, and accordingly 65 per cent of turnover must be derived from the sale of donated goods. Confusion exists over this figure, as some people believe that the turnover of bought-in goods could be up to 49 per cent and that the requirement is simply that the shop sells 'mainly' donated goods (Horne and Broadbridge 1993, 1995). Originally covered by the 1967 General Rate Act and subsequently amended by the 1988 Local Government Finance Act (LGFA), which introduced the Community Charge and the Uniform Business Rate, charity shops are covered by section 64 (10) of this 1988 Act. The Act states that a hereditment (property) is to be treated as being for charitable purposes if it is 'wholly or mainly used for the sale of goods donated to a charity and the proceeds of the sale of the goods (after the deduction of any expenses) are applied for the purpose of the charity'. The term 'mainly' is open to interpretation and causes much confusion.

If the merchandise mix is a key determinant for rate relief, then it would be logical to assume that shops in Category III (100 per cent new goods) have no such relief. Research suggests, however, that some shops in this category are nevertheless granted tax relief (Horne and Broadbridge 1995). This confusion over trading legislation suggests that charity retailing is moving faster than the imposition of legislation.

Until 1988 little thought was given as to whether charities indulging in retail activities were to be considered to be trading in the real sense. In section 505 of the Income and Corporation Taxes Act 1988 the exemption from tax given to charities extends to income from trade only if that trade is the primary purpose of the charity. There are also exemptions for certain trading activities that are not covered by statute, the most important being that relating to the sale of donated goods. If goods are donated to a charity, their sale is deemed to be the realisation of a gift and not the act of trading. This would suggest that a charity shop selling 100 per cent donated goods is considered not to be trading but to be realising the value of gifts. This interpretation still applies even if that gift is cleaned or renovated. However, if the renovation is significant, or if it changes the nature of the good, then the sale will amount to a trade. Presumably therefore if cushion covers, say, are made out of donated second-hand curtains, they are to be considered 'new goods'.

Category III comprises charities that sell only new bought-in goods. They entered the market selling only new goods and most sell goods that are related in some way to the charity. Examples include the National Trust, which sells products related to individual properties as well as more general goods, and Camphill Village Trust, which sells own-produced goods. Some are highly specialised retailers selling customer-specific goods; for example, the Royal Air Force (RAF) Association sells RAF-related products that are bought by ex-RAF/WAAF service personnel. The Royal National Institute for the Blind (RNIB) has outlets stocked with goods specific to the needs of customers with a visual handicap, and similarly the Scout Association sells a range of

Table 2.2 Category III shops ranked by total income

Charity	Shop nos.	Volunteers	Annual wage bill (£)	Total income (£)
National Trust (Eng.) Ltd	281	—	4,707,100	22,205,000
Cards for Good Causes	279	6,005	—	5,316,000
Royal Society for the Protection of Birds (RSPB)	13	20	336,328	2,388,972
National Trust Scotland	41	23	542,138	3,011,672
Royal National Lifeboat Institution (RNLI)	118	1,180	—	1,945,066

Source: Horne (2000)

equipment and clothing relating to Scouting activity (Corporate Intelligence 1992). It could be argued that many have a captive market because of their location, and it is interesting that, on the whole, the general public do not perceive these shops as charity shops (Phelan 1994). The fortunes of these new goods shops fluctuate more obviously than those selling donated goods. Phelan suggested a downturn in their profit margins in his 1998 publication but recorded good news from this sector of the charity shop market in 1999, with a 5.7 per cent increase in their total sales and a 12 per cent growth in profits (Phelan 1996). Table 2.2 shows the 'top five' Category III charity shop operations.

Classification by merchandise mix helps to sort and to clarify some of the anomalies of the charity shop. Table 2.2 categorises still further those shops in Category III by ranking them in terms of their overall income. This total income is another way of classifying charity shops within the three sectors identified on p. 20.

Another means of classification is by cause type. The only way that this is used at present is in the categorisation of hospice shops. These are by nature often small retail charities operating one or two shops in a local area, although some operate chains of up to twenty-one shops (St Peter's Hospice, Bristol, for example). Although the topic is unresearched, anecdotal evidence suggests that there is a very close relationship between the local community and its hospice shop. Loyal communities support their local hospice by means of donations and purchase of goods. Because of the nature of a hospice as a home for the care of the terminally ill, the disposal of goods after bereavement can often be very traumatic and the hospice shop is a comfortable way of accomplishing this disposal (see Chapter 4).

Raison d'être: conflict between social function and commercial enterprise

One major difficulty that many charities entering the retail arena face is that of 'What business are we in?' If we look back to the origins of the shops, there was an element of social welfare and opportunism – the 'raising of the submerged' and the prospect of proselytising – but as the economic potential of the shops became evident, commercialisation and profit making became a main reason for selling goods. Most charities go into retailing in order to make money, which will in turn enable them to carry out their individual, primary purpose such as the relief of poverty, the advancement of education, the promoting of religion or other purposes presumed to be beneficial to the community (*Charities Digest* 1995). This can cause tension within the charity shop organisation (see Chapters 5 and 7 and Goodall 2000c) and between charity shops and their local shoppers (Maddrell 2000). One major charity suggests that compromise is needed, as there is conflict with hard business and charity. Its mission statement for trading is 'to generate as much money as possible without compromising its charitable aims' (interview with charity fundraiser).

Dees (1998) suggests that conflict can occur between the culture of the commercial world and that of the voluntary sector and that many of those who work in the voluntary sector find commercialism an uncomfortable bedfellow. Charities are not always clear as to why they entered the retail sector, and the purposes of the shop are often multiple. The perceptions of the shop's functions can be varied, with headquarters managers and 'shop floor' volunteers seeing them from very different perspectives. Figure 2.1 indicates a range of purpose from that of purely social to that of purely commercial and suggests a continuum of purpose between the two (Horne 2000). This continuum highlights the complexity of the charity shop: it is not necessarily market driven or solely a 'social service', but, depending on merchandise, customer base, staff and location, operates in a multifunctional way. It is suggested (Horne 2000) that the charity shop performs interrelated functions. The first of these, and the main *raison d'être* for the majority of charity shops, is to provide a method of raising unallocated funds that can be used for any purpose and are not constrained by, for example, the will of a corporate or individual donor.

The amount of money raised by individual shops depends on their location, the quality of goods sold and the pricing policy, as well as the dedication and professionalism of the staff and management. Phelan *et al.* (1998) suggest that in 1998, 6,238 shops run by 82

	Methods	Social service orientation	← →	Commercial service orientation
S t a k e h o l d e r s		Social service social value	Mixed motives mission- and market-driven social and economic value	Market-driven economic value
	Customer	Pay under market value prices	Subsidised to mixed commercial prices	Market rate competitive prices
	Workforce	Volunteer/ community service	Mixed volunteers and paid staff	Salaried staff market rate pay scales
	Donors/ suppliers	Goods donated	Donated goods and bought-in goods	Market rate prices
	Local authority	Subsidised business rate	Mixture of mandatory and discretionary rates	Full local authority rates paid

Figure 2.1 Charity shop purpose: social to commercial orientation

Source: Horne (2000)

charities raised a total net income in excess of £91 million on a turn-over of £365 million. Taking the largest charity shops (ranked by income), but excluding gift shops and hospice shops (Phelan *et al.* 1998), the total income from 5,282 shops was £308,856,951. The expenditure on this sum was £230,850,458, giving an overall profit of £78,006,493 and a profit margin of 25.1 per cent on turnover. However, as can be seen from Table 2.3, the margin varies from charity to charity.

In 1999 there was an overall increase of 38 shops, resulting in an income of £338,975,656 from a total of 5,818 shops. Although this represented an increase of 2.6 per cent on 1998 figures, the overall pro-fits fell to £62,808,135, suggesting that increased costs were part of the explanation for the changing fate of the sector – although one has to be aware of the limitations of this survey, as well as of interpreting aggregated figures from charities with very diverse retail practices. With many different accounting methods and structures in operation, it is difficult to compare profitability. For example, charities vary the amounts of capital employed and headquarters' overheads.

The second perceived function of the charity shop is to provide a social service, offering cheap goods to those customers who cannot afford to shop at commercial retail outlets. These shops also offer a cheap alternative to those who, although not on or below the poverty line, are able to extend a very limited income by purchasing second-hand clothes and household goods, and to those who are simply

Table 2.3 Incomes generated by top ten charities

Charity	Date figures prep. to	Income total (£)	Average profit per shop per week (£)	Profit as a percentage of turnover	Wage bill as percentage of total income	Average sales per shop per week (£)	Donated goods as percentage of turnover
Oxfam	30.4.99	57,084,000	365	27.3	13.8	1,331	82
ICRF	1.09.98	31,323,948	131	10.5	17.6	1,289	75
British Heart Foundation	28.3.98	35,696,759	555	27.6	NA	1,879	NA
SCOPE	31.3.99	27,060,002	544	30.6	31.0	1,680	98
Barnardo's	31.3.99	22,039,512	347	26.4	33.5	1,297	86
Help the Aged	30.4.99	27,795,000	366	24.3	42.0	1,432	95
Cancer Research Campaign	31.3.99	19,239,670	352	24.9	22.7	1,462	98
Age Concern, all shops	31.3.99	11,637,983	27	4.3	29.1	556	96
British Red Cross	31.12.98	15,503,937	215	31.6	NA	682	99
Save the Children Fund	31.3.99	6,727,172	325	37.5	7.4	842	69

Source: Horne (2000)

Note: NA, not available

'thrifty'. While almost all charity shops offer this service to a degree, those emphasising service to their locality are, for the most part, situated in 'poorer' locations in areas where customers can access them easily. There is evidence to suggest that these 'community'-based shops become part of the community, acting as a base for meeting friends and sharing problems (see Chapters 3, 5 and 7).

As well as selling goods for profit and acting as a 'social service', the third function of the charity shop is to raise public awareness of its particular charitable cause. A shop in a location with good footfall will attract the attention of passers-by and thus can be used as a place to disseminate information, to display the logo and to promote the charity's name. It can be used as a meeting place for volunteer recruitment and, of course, donations of both goods and money can be made there. However, this third function of charity shops is often a by-product rather than an explicit aim, with many charity shops focusing on trading virtually to the exclusion of disseminating the charity message. When this occurs, it is a lost opportunity for both the charity itself and potential users of the charity.

These three functions are those most commonly thought of in relation to the charity shop, but a fourth function can be seen: that of the recycling of goods, or the 'green' function. Charity shops serve to recycle goods on two levels (Horne 1998). The first is that of goods which are unwanted by one set of consumers being offered for sale to another set which is ready to buy. The second is the recycling of goods at the end of their current usefulness, and thus saleability in that form, into a new and resaleable form, for example the conversion of clothing via ragging merchants into stuffing for car upholstery, paper-making and new fabric. One charity shop manager said of dubious-quality clothing, 'If in doubt, rag it' (Manager F, Oxford). For many charity shops this approach was taken even further, with some charities now purposefully collecting rags and selling them on to rag merchants at a profit (although the market for rags has been susceptible to price fluctuations in recent years). In a further twist, a very small number of charities without charity shops began to license rag merchants to collect goods in their name in return for a payment per tonne of goods collected (Phelan 1998) (see Chapter 4 for a fuller discussion of this). The green function is often overlooked both by the charities and the consumers. In an age where 'green issues' are at the front of policy making there is often surprisingly little effort made by charities to appeal to the 'green consumer' to patronise the stores – another lost opportunity.

Different combinations of these four functions of the charity shop place individual shops and chains in different positions on the continuum from the social service orientation through to that of commercial orientation, from 'community service' to that of 'pure' fundraiser, with some charities changing location on the continuum over time. The majority of charities now view the primary function of the charity shop as that of fund-raiser.

Competition

With a rapidly increasing number of charity shops, competition becomes fierce, and in these circumstances understanding customer behaviour is of paramount importance inasmuch as the success of the organisation depends on it (Kotler and Andreasen, 1991). It is also believed that the better the marketers understand their customers' needs and wants through purchasing behaviour, the better they will be able to meet these needs and wants (Foxall and Goldsmith, 1994). Added to this, 'selling objectives for a retail operation also requires a good understanding of an organisation's customers' (Lovelock and Weinberg, 1983). This customer knowledge also improves and enables nurturing of the long-term commitment of the donors to the organisation (Guy and Patton, 1989).

Increased professionalism can be identified in the retailing practice of many charity shops. This has been characterised by the use of paid staff – professionals – and applying business practices (Goodall 2000c), probably the most widespread being indeed that of the introduction of paid management with retail experience, which is now seen in the top retailing charities. Given that raising money is the primary reason for the majority of the charity retail sector to be in business, it is not surprising that this sector has become increasingly professional in its retail practice (see Chapter 5). This increase in professional practice has brought more revenue to the charities concerned but has also brought problems, the most obvious of which is that of competition, which manifests itself differently depending in which category the shop operates (Horne and Broadbridge 1995).

In order to put this debate about professionalisation into a theoretical context, the cyclical retail model known as the Wheel of Retailing can be used to demonstrate how professionalisation can change the purpose of a charity shop, as well as suggesting possible post-professionalisation scenarios, including the opportunity for new charity retailers to enter the market.

Charity shops and the Wheel of Retailing

The Wheel of Retailing, although limited as a working model of retailing evolution, does serve to describe a progress of growth and development. Developed by McNair in 1958, it has been a topic of argument and discussion ever since – for example, see Hollander (1960), Savitt (1988), Gipsrud (1986) and D'Amico (1983), and demonstrations of its use by Bucklin (1972) and Brown (1990, 1992). In 1958 McNair described a cycle in distribution as a wheel that 'always revolves, sometimes slowly, sometimes more rapidly but does not stand still'. He recognised the circular nature of some types of retailing where the original concept has moved on and developed to a point where the niche initially exploited has been left so far behind that it is no longer occupied. If the niche is still valid and relevant, it is to be expected that others will fill it.

Incomers attract the public on the basis of low price appeal, which is made possible by low operating costs. As they progress, they trade up, seeking greater respectability. McNair suggests that if after the trading up process they are still in business, there will be a period of growth when business will be taken away from the established retailers who have clung to their old methods. During the process of growth the institution becomes respectable in terms of the customers, potential customers and investors. With this movement upwards the capital investment increases, as do the operating costs. It is at this point that the maturity stage is reached. The premises are probably now larger, with more elaborate fixtures and fittings, and greater promotional efforts are undertaken. At this stage the competition is with other similar institutions rather than with 'old-line' competitors. The maturity phase is followed by one of top-heaviness and decline in return on investment and eventual vulnerability. This vulnerability is the next revolution of the wheel and the point at which the next entrepreneur starts a low-cost business and slips into the opening. From this simplistic hypothesis the wheel has been tidied up by Hollander (1960) and re-turned by McNair and May (1978) when they expanded the original theory by saying that in the USA the cyclical process both quickened and affected an increasing number of retail sectors. Taking the suggestion of Brown (1990) that some of the most prominent retail institutions have reflected the wheel theory, the simple McNair (1958) description of the wheel can be compared to the development of the charity shop.

Thus a charity shop operating primarily as a social service to its local area and with modest fund-raising expectations is going to be

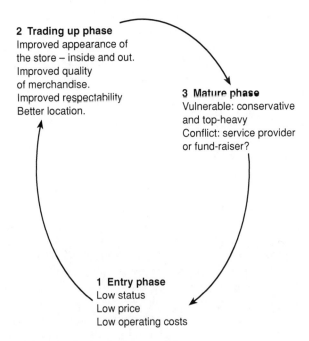

2 Trading up phase
Improved appearance of
the store – inside and out.
Improved quality
of merchandise.
Improved respectability
Better location.

3 Mature phase
Vulnerable: conservative
and top-heavy
Conflict: service provider
or fund-raiser?

1 Entry phase
Low status
Low price
Low operating costs

Figure 2.2 The Wheel of Retailing

Source: Horne (2000)

located in a secondary, if not poor, location. The price of its goods
will reflect the limited expenditure capability of its customers, and
often these goods are recycled within this customer segment. For
example, baby clothes are donated to the shop from outside the community, purchased by local customers used and re-donated to be sold
on until no longer in a fit state for resale (McNair 1958). Because of
the social function of the shop, profits are minimal and the whole
operation is that displayed in Phase 1 of the Wheel (Figure 2.2) – that
is, low status, low price and low operating costs. The goods are all
donated, the shop's emphasis is on service to the community and it is
managed and staffed by volunteers, with no, or little, independent,
centralised management.

As the realisation of fund-raising potential occurs, so 'trading up'
takes place. Shops are opened in better secondary or in primary locations. Greater resources are put into collecting and presenting for sale
good-quality donated goods. Consideration is given to store layout
and to corporate colours and logos. It is at this stage that new goods
might be bought in to broaden the merchandise range and widen the

customer base, and paid managers introduced. It could be argued that at present all charity shops in all stages of maturity continue to display some element of social service. By their affiliation to a charity, all shops act as an advertisement to the general public as well as providing a focal point for 'drop in' information, volunteer recruitment and information distribution. However, as the charity retail operation moves 'around the Wheel', so it is potentially distanced from those in society who can afford only to shop at the 'community' charity shop, thus creating an interesting example of potential social exclusion within the sector (see Chapter 6 on pricing).

In Phase 2 of the Wheel the emphasis is on fund-raising rather than social service, with new goods bought in to maintain stock levels and to broaden the merchandise range. These new goods add further dimensions of customer service such as the provision of fair trade goods. A wider merchandise range also serves to widen the customer base, as does the improved respectability of the shop as the concept of 'trading up' occurs. We now have not only a continuum of charity shop purpose (see Figure 2.2), but also a continuum of customers ranging from those able to shop only in the cheap and basic Phase 1 shops for functional goods to those looking for a bargain or 'collectable', or those positional shoppers wanting to purchase new goods in order to support a specific charity or the concept of fair trade in Phase 2 shops.

McNair (1958) postulates that as a result of trading up, the new institution becomes 'mature' and is now top-heavy, conservative and unable to show a good rate of return on investment. Certainly the charities with the greatest investment and return from their shops are the largest and have had criticism levelled at them for being too large and 'top-heavy'. In principle the very nature of these charitable organisations defies the concept of bureaucracy and lack of good return on investment, but in practice the differential between turnover and profits – and indeed falling profits – suggests an alternative scenario. The mature stage of bureaucracy and 'top-heaviness' could be used to describe those charities with the largest number of shops. These chains operate with retail departments and a hierarchy of retail management. Arguably these 'mature' charity retailers/chains are already professional retailers rather than charities. Oxfam price tags illustrating how the cost of the item bought might be used to buy seeds, etc. are an example of an attempt explicitly to link fund-raising and the purpose of the charity.

The concept of a constantly turning wheel implies that retail organisations that have evolved to a mature state will gradually revert to the initial, Phase 1, trading style. This is unrealistic and rarely happens, although some highly structured charity retail chains have recently devolved greater autonomy to the local level on matters such as pricing and display in order to increase turnover in the face of recent stagnation in, or saturation of, the sector. In reality, organisations trade up, leaving a niche for new companies to enter, since, as McNair (1958) suggests, eventually the retail institution emerges as a high-cost, high-status establishment whose sales policy is based on quality and service rather than price. These high-margin operators are then vulnerable to new competitors who enter the market as low-status retailers. The new companies are not necessarily competitors until they invade the niche of the matured company.

There is little competitive overlap between a well-organised chain of charity retailers with professional management and a reliance on sourcing new goods, and a single, locally organised charity shop relying on donated goods and dedicated amateurs. Therefore, as charity shops mature, the initial niche is indeed left open. This is true only to the extent that the mature chain does not continue to predate the second-hand, donated goods market. Since there frequently is little sign of a change in specialisation in the products sold as the Wheel progresses to maturity, the newcomer competing locally with a Phase 3 outlet would be faced with finding its own niche in the goods offered, either by generating its own 'niche' support network or perhaps as a specialist shop offering very low-cost goods or specialist goods. However, specialisation is also a route being adopted by charity chains in Phase 3 mode, such as Oxfam furniture shops and bookshops. While charity retailers have successfully entered this specialist niche market, they often compete with other second-hand shops.

Staff and cyclical change

The low-cost operation of the initial entry into the retail market can be identified through the use of a totally volunteer workforce. Most charities start their retail activity with unpaid managers and floor staff. As the number of stores increases, the locations improve and the merchandise requires more careful selection and detailed accounting, the need for more professional paid staff increases. At present the majority of paid staff are at managerial level and the 'workforce' is still mainly voluntary (see Chapter 5).

The logical progression through the Wheel model would suggest a movement from part-time volunteering to paid full-time staff. Freathy (1997) suggests that in commercial retailing, at each segment of the Wheel a transformation of labour relationships can be identified, from flexibility of small independent shops through to formal and centralised structures of retailers at the 'mature' stage. Although no specific research has tested this in the charity sector, work by Maddrell (1999, 2000) and Whithear (1999) would suggest that for most charity retailers this is not the case and that the part-time and flexible nature of the volunteer workforce is evident through to the 'mature' stage.

Whithear (1999) gives interesting insights into volunteering in a charity shop, and to the differences found in the volunteer force in shops with paid managers as opposed to those with volunteer managers. His findings suggest that the volunteer managers had a sales force whose members were older, had less retail experience and were longer-serving than those in shops managed by paid managers. While the 'professional' managers wanted a more 'professional' team, which would work standard hours, in contrast the volunteer managers were more 'accepting' of the volunteers and accepted their need to work as a group. However, it is wrong to characterise 'professional' and 'voluntary' as diametrically opposed. There is a middle way to be found in many charity shops in the form of 'professional voluntarism' that aims to raise funds at the same time as working with and valuing volunteer input (Goodall 2000c). Contrary to the perceptions often held that store service levels are low, the quality of customer service in many charity shops appears to be high (Maddrell 2000). The Sue Ryder management insists that every customer must be made to feel welcome, cherished and important ('High street charity' 1992).

As purpose becomes more commercial in nature, so the change manifests itself in a greater professionalisation of operations, and at this stage the retail operations match or indeed surpass those in commercial organisations. The shops run by the National Trust, for example, are run as mainstream retailers and are often not recognised as charity shops by the public. Competitive mainstream retailers have copied elements of their format. An example is the Past Times chain, who realise the potential of this traditional/nostalgic market.

The areas of competition, for customers, goods and volunteers, could be described as 'internal' problems that are part of the retail operations of charity shops, but a different level of competition that is beyond the control of the charity retailer has become an issue that could, in the long run, have a hugely detrimental effect on certain charity shops, namely competition perceived by established retailers. This is causing much concern throughout the country, and might have severe repercussions for charity shops if legislation were to be brought in, say, to add VAT to the sale of donated goods. This perceived competition by small established retailers manifests itself in the belief of the Federation of Small Businesses that charity shops trade on an unfair footing, gaining benefit from their charitable status (Federation of Small Businesses (FSB) 1995). There is a feeling among retailers and local chambers of commerce that tension is growing and that in a time of recession the established retailer will fight for the right to operate regardless of the fact that the competition might be fundraising for a worthy cause. Some retailers are registering complaints with chambers of commerce and the Office of Fair Trading alleging unfair competition. Most of the debate of established retailers against charity retailers has been directed to the issue of rates paid or not paid and the fact that charity shops have few overheads, either fixed or unfixed. Another issue that has not been so well argued is that if a charity is given rate relief, it can then afford to pay higher rent and rates for a property than an established retailer and this, in many cases, serves to keep rent and rates in a given locality at a higher level than would otherwise be sustained.

It has been suggested by many established retailers that the mandatory relief should apply only to those shops selling 100 per cent donated goods. Obviously those charities that follow such a strategy are happy with the proposal. Many charities are denied the discretionary award, and some authorities have refused the mandatory one on terms of unfair competition if the proportion of new goods is very high. There is a suggestion that the percentage of mandatory relief should be brought down from 80 per cent to 50 per cent, which, as Phelan in 1998 pointed out, would have cost Oxfam, at that time, approximately £1 million across its chain of 844 shops.

The rise in the number of charity shops, together with the change in their image and their move away from poor secondary trading sites to primary high street sites and even, occasionally, a site in a shopping centre, has made some established retailers fear the proliferation of charity shops. There is evidence to suggest that some chambers of commerce are putting pressure on local councils to go so far as to restrict the number of successful charity shop applications (Horne 1995). The following quotations are emblematic of alternative perspectives on this debate nation-wide:

> 'The expansion of charity shops is an enormous problem which has caused the local economy to suffer due to lost rates, employment and business impact – as charity shops proliferate the negative drain on the economy increases.'
>
> (Spokesperson from the Federation of Small Businesses, Scotland)

'There are far too many charity shops, but better a charity shop than a boarded up shop.'

(Shopkeeper 9, Stirling)

The increasing number is not the only problem perceived by established retailers. Complaints are made regarding the competition because of the increased sophistication of their operations and because of the change in the merchandise mix offered by charity retailers. Some retailers have been so annoyed by the alteration of the merchandise mix by charity shops that they have ceased to deal with suppliers who supply charity shops. A further insult to injury was the case of a loyal customer who requested the name and address of a supplier in order to recommend it to a charity retailer, much to the chagrin of the shopkeeper, who resented the fact that the charity could then 'sell the product at little more than cost instead of the recommended retail price' (Shopkeeper 4, Inverness).

Some retailers deal with the situation by offering better value for money or by stocking different products from those sold in the charity shops. Although many of these problems of similar stock do not affect the small shopkeeper, the majority do feel the perceived competition.

'We would like to see restrictions on rate relief for charity shops.'

(Shopkeeper 1, Inverness)

'The fact that these shops get so much help in terms of rate relief, a volunteer workforce, etc. upsets small businesses, especially in times of hardship when all are struggling; it's deemed to be an unfair advantage and we would like to see restriction on rate relief for charity shops.'

(Shopkeeper 1, Inverness)

Comments such as these illustrate small retailers' strong feelings, though many say that they have no objections to the 'genuine thrift shops'. There is, however, evidence to suggest that there is a degree of mutuality between mainstream retailers and charity retailers, and some suggestion that the charity retailer provides 'added value' to the wider retail environment (Paddison 2000). The level of competition is also in part determined by the economic well-being of the area. For example, in Oxford a jeweller sends pensioners around the corner to buy silver-plated frames at a cheaper price in the charity shop. Even so, there is every reason to suppose that competition between charities for goods, workforce and customers, will continue to increase, as will competition, perceived or otherwise, with established retailers, particularly as charity shops 'trade up'. These issues will be revisited in the following chapters in relation to shoppers, donors, staffing and the pricing of goods.

3   Customers and demand
Thrift, lifestyle, convenience and coming out of the cold

This chapter is concerned with the shoppers in charity shops, the consumers. Consumption has been shown to be a complex matter, relating to gender, class, race, age and cross-cutting interests such as 'tribe', fashion or lifestyle, as well as socio-economic reality (despite the spread of credit), political or moral influences, filtered through the lens of identity and associated aspirations and fears (see Chapter 1). Sites of consumption seem to have pervaded almost all aspects of social life (Shields 1992), as consumption takes place not only in shops, department stores, malls and markets but also in public buildings, museums, heritage sites, places of worship and through the internet and mass media. Indeed, Bauman (1990: 204 cited by Lury 1999: 49) suggests that consumption so dominates modern society that individuals engage in 'translating the task of learning the art of living as . . . shopping skills and purchasing power'. This increased visibility of different forms of shopping is accompanied by other characteristics of contemporary consumption, such as increased credit availability, increased interest in collecting as an activity, shopping-related illnesses and the political organisation of and by consumers (Lury 1999). Each of these relates in different ways to the experience of shopping in a charity shop as a specific site of consumption, and will be referenced in relation to the consumption motivations, lifestyle aspirations and intentions for goods acquired on the part of shoppers using this form of retail outlet. This can be summed up in the deceptively simple and all-encompassing question: why shop in a charity shop?

Shoppers have been categorised into five psychological types representing attitudes towards, sites of and practices of consumption: alternative shoppers (12 per cent), routine shoppers (31 per cent), leisure shoppers (24 per cent), careful shoppers (15 per cent) and thrifty shoppers (18 per cent) (Lunt and Livingstone 1992). The largest group are the 'routine shoppers', who generally shop on the high street.

They take little pleasure in shopping as a practice, rarely buy on impulse or use alternative forms of shopping, and generally seem disengaged from consumer culture. There is little to suggest that shoppers with this profile are likely to patronise charity shops, as is also the case with the 'careful shoppers', who while careful and economical in their consumption, focus on the use value of the goods and generally avoid alternative retail opportunities. Leisure shoppers, identified by Lunt and Livingstone as the second largest group of shoppers, are *potential* users of charity shops as they enjoy a range of shopping experiences and use consumer goods as rewards, promises and bribes in social relations. However, in contrast to leisure shoppers, who are closest to the stereotypical shopper, it is the 'alternative' and 'thrifty' shoppers who are most likely to use charity shops as a regular site of consumption (representing a total of 30 per cent of shoppers in this characterisation). 'Alternative' shoppers use the alternative market including charity shops, jumble sales, second-hand shops and markets, but take little pleasure in shopping *per se* and 'seem to stand outside the pressures and pleasures of modern consumer culture' (Lury 1999: 235). In shopping for the best buy, 'thrifty' shoppers use all forms of consumption opportunity from the high street to the alternative market, for example waiting for the seasonal sales to purchase a desired new good such as a mattress. These consumers take some pleasure in shopping, including shopping as a family outing (Lunt and Livingstone 1992) (so may overlap with 'leisure' shoppers in their use of charity shops). While this classification is inevitably limiting, not least in ascribing consumers to one particular category when an individual's consumption practices may vary over time, space and type of shopping (e.g. when on holiday or when purchasing consumer durables compared to regular provisioning), it is a useful starting point when considering the consumption motivations and practices of those using charity shops.

Who shops in charity shops?

Attitudes to buying second-hand clothes have become significantly more positive in recent years, and this rehabilitation is attributable, at least in part, to their availability in the relatively formal setting of high street charity shops, coupled with evolving discourses of thrift and environmental stewardship. As one of the catalysts in this change of attitude, the charity shop sector has also been a major beneficiary of the reduced stigma attached to buying second-hand goods, and especially clothes (Mintel 1997).

Nationally, it is estimated that 60 per cent of women and 36 per cent of men use charity shops at least occasionally, with 27 per cent of women and 12 per cent of men using them regularly or often (Mintel 1997). The figures for regular or frequent users broadly mirror Lunt and Livingstone's estimates of alternative and thrifty shoppers, but the high degree of at least occasional use found in this survey suggests a much wider market base than Lunt and Livingstone's alternative and thrifty shoppers, particularly in the case of women. There is clearly the potential for an expanded market if the sector were able to encourage more frequent use on the part of those using charity shops 'rarely' or 'occasionally' – especially men. However, there are complex variations in use of charity shops by region and social class as well as by gender, variations that are significant to our understanding of the place of charity shop consumption in relation to identity and economic empowerment.

The Mintel (1997) report suggests that there are regional differences in levels of use, the lowest being in Scotland (15 per cent of respondents) and the highest in the south of England, where 25 per cent of respondents shop in charity shops. This overall (slight) inverse North–South divide in use patterns, which is contrary to broad patterns of economic wealth, might be accounted for by a higher density of charity shops in the South (Mintel 1997).

In a survey of 236 general shoppers on the high street in Oxford (Maddrell 2001a), 65 per cent of respondents were users of charity shops. A distinction was found in terms of gender, with 74 per cent of women using charity shops, compared with 53 per cent of men. No age group of female respondents fell below 62 per cent patronising charity outlets, but perhaps surprisingly, the oldest age group of women (the over 60 years) were the only group to have this lowest rate of participation as 'charity shoppers'. In contrast, 100 per cent of the 51- to 60-year group of women used charity shops (see Table 3.1).

Table 3.1 Women's use of charity shops by age group (Oxford)

Age	Percentage of age group using charity shops
18–30	77
31–40	66
41–50	80
51–60	100
60 plus	62

Source: Maddrell (2000)

Interestingly, men showed much less variation with age in their use of charity shops, with approximately 50 per cent of men each age group using charity shops, rising to 60 per cent for both categories over 51 years. Also, significantly, this suggests an equivalent patronage of charity shops by men and women in the over-60 age group. The relatively high use (77 per cent) of charity shops by women in the 18–30 age group perhaps reflects the high proportion of students in the Oxford sample, compared to 50 per cent of women in this age group in the Isle of Man, for example (Maddrell 2001b). Similarly, a rate of 50 per cent participation by male respondents in the same age group is relatively high compared with that found in some other surveys (e.g. Parsons 2000, who found that fewer than 3 per cent of in-shop questionnaire respondents were men under 35 years of age) – but only slightly higher than the 45 per cent of men of the same age group in the Isle of Man. All surveys to date show higher use of charity shops as a site of consumption for women than for men, suggesting a continued gendered character to this consumption space.

Figures from the Mintel Retail Intelligence report on charity shops (1997) suggest that on a nation-wide aggregation in the UK there is a strong correlation between use of charity shops and social class. ABs (professionals) are the lowest users at 15 per cent, rising to 17 per cent for C1 and C2s, and there is a significant rise in use by the lower-income groups, with 25 per cent of Ds and 30 per cent of Es using charity shops. While suggesting on one level a clear relationship between class and consumption in charity shops, the figures themselves challenge the stereotype of the charity shop as the preserve of the poor, as 15 per cent of ABs *do* buy goods and *only* 30 per cent of those on the lowest incomes choose to purchase goods in charity shops. Charity shops are now used by consumers from all socio-economic backgrounds, but findings also suggest that the most regular customers are from lower socio-economic groups (Mintel 1997) and that less than half of charity shoppers are in some form of paid work (Parsons 2000). It is important to remember that there are different product offerings within and between charity shops, accommodating very different consumption experiences and practices. This differentiated clientele is identified by one manager:

'We've got two distinct types of clientele: 75 per cent are the single parents, unemployed, pensioners, low waged – and some dealers; the rest are real yuppies – they spend quite a lot of money, but are more particular about the quality of the goods.'

(Manager V, Oxford)

Establishing a regular and even 'brand-loyal' clientele is something that is becoming sought after by charity retailers in an increasingly competitive marketplace. Some charities (such as Barnardo's) have piloted loyalty reward points cards like those used in supermarkets and DIY stores. Findings in the Oxford survey suggest that half of shoppers have a degree of loyalty to particular charities, in both their purchasing and their donation habits, but the ethos of 'supporting' a charity is more likely to affect donations than consumption. Thirty-five per cent of consumer–donors donate to specific charities but purchase goods from a number of charity outlets, with only 8 per cent buying from a single charity shop (or charity brand). The questions of why people shop in charity outlets and what they buy are central to understanding the market base and the role of charity shops in consumption culture, as well as aspects of their socio-economic functions for consumers.

Thrift, lifestyle, convenience and coming out of the cold: why people shop in charity shops

Consumers have varied motives when they approach the charity shop as a consumption space. The thrifty (a category that, Miller (1998) suggests, accounts for most of us) are looking, out of necessity or desire, for a bargain. The elderly or those with limited mobility appreciate the convenience of a local shop. Those whose lifestyle choices prioritise ethical trading or sustainable development seek fair trade or recycled goods, while others (or maybe the same) consumers seek material goods of individuality and, some would argue, authenticity. For some the charity shop can be a source of sociability or even a place of sociation, a regular meeting place. It can also be a site of leisure, blending leisure with consumption, as has been noted historically in the case of department stores (see Domosh 1996), and more recently associated with the experience of malls (see Shields 1992) and of spectacle in car boot fairs (see Stone *et al.* 1996; Gregson and Crewe 1997a). These complex influences can distinguish different types of consumers, as well as interact within one person's motivations, which may vary over time, seasonally, with changing life cycles or as experience of charity shop consumption grows, fears are overcome and knowledge of the range of goods grows. For example, those with limited mobility and financial resources may find the charity shop an opportunity for affordable and accessible leisure browsing as well as a convenient staging post when out shopping, as in the case of one Oxford suburb:

'The Age Concern bus drops the elderly near the library and post office on pension day and they come in [to the charity shop opposite] while they're waiting for the library to open. They look around, maybe buy a few things.'

(Manager O, Oxford)

When asked to categorise their reasons for using charity shops for consumption, Oxford charity shopper respondents identified *low prices* as the primary motive (65 per cent of men and 55 per cent of women), but this was closely followed by a *desire to support (the) charity* (51 per cent of women and 38 per cent of men). Arguably this could be described as 'double whammy feelgood' consumption, combining thrift with a sense of supporting charity. The attraction of the *possibility of finding unusual goods* appealed primarily to both men and women of the 18–30 age group, although it was also a significant factor for women aged 31–40. These are consumers looking for non-mainstream cultural goods as markers of their individuality, including those looking for retro fashion, household goods and clothing items. *Local convenience* was the least-cited motive but was significant for a quarter of women aged 31–40 and over 60 years of age. Eighteen to thirty years was the only male age group for which local convenience was a significant reason for purchasing goods from a charity shop. While not numerically significant, two individual shoppers' responses shed light on alternative personal motives. One male respondent (18–30 years of age) cited the *opportunity to purchase fair trade products* (notably consumables such as tea and coffee) as an important factor influencing his purchasing patterns in charity shops, suggesting positional consumption practices based on ethical decisions. Another man in the 60-plus age bracket described himself as an 'opportunist' attracted by the *quality of items* in the charity shop (implicitly in relation to price and the possibility of direct or indirect profit from the purchase).

While purpose-built retail parks, malls and shopping centres have the functional attractions such as ease of access, wide choice and lower prices, 'for all consumption sites these benefits are quickly outstripped by the symbolic and social value . . . as a site of communication and interaction' (Shields 1992: 5). This social value of communication and interaction is a significant element of the charity shop's offering. Just as social relationships can be developed between common groups of consumers, a different sort of relationship can be developed between those running the shop and their customers, particularly regular customers. In *haute couture* and, to a lesser degree, ready-to-wear clothes, a salesperson can form an intimate knowledge of a regular client's style and self-presentation, knowing which lines fall within that client's configuration of style, acting as both audience and gatekeeper for the client (Huat Chua 1992). This seems a long way from the charity shop consumer, but in practice there are several similarities between Huat Chua's study of women's fashion in Singapore and observed and reported experiences of shopping in charity shops. These include almost daily visits by some customers, often browsing rather than buying; the use of the shop as a meeting place by clients moving in the same social circles; as well as the development of salesperson–client relationships that can influence client choice.

Many charity shop managers report having daily visits from a number of customers (including dealers scouting for goods for resale). Customers are attracted by the possibility of unpredictable and eclectic stock in both general and specialist charity shops: 'Some people haunt the place. If we're closed for a holiday there are streams of customers the next day' (Manager K, Oxford). Daily visits have also been recorded by Parsons' (2000) Bristol survey of charity shoppers. Shopping addiction has emerged in recent years as a serious psychological problem (two Oxford managers expressed concern about specific customers regularly spending beyond their means), and this syndrome clearly could affect charity shop customers, and is not necessarily any the less significant just because of the cheaper prices. Weaker versions of habit and the high of the bargain hunt are certainly apparent in some charity shop customers, demonstrated by one customer: 'I'm just coming in for my fix, I can't pass without coming in. Have you got any new handbags?' (Customer 3, Oxford O).

Regular customers can also be motivated not only by the thrill of the unpredictable consumption opportunity, but by the sense of sociability they find in charity shops, where they may be known by name, and interest taken in them as both individuals and consumers. There are clearly bands of regular customers attached to many charity shops for whom the shop is a place of sociability and sociation:

> 'We have daily customers, people we're on first name terms with, but lots of people use it as a social place. I told the doctor's wife, "Just come in for a chat, you don't need to buy anything," Others meet before work for a quick look, then dash back at lunchtime to buy.'
>
> (Manager I, Oxford)

Some charity shop managers are conscious of the social needs of their clientele, see this as part of their broad 'charity' role and deliberately take steps to address these in their approach to managing their shop:

> 'Quite a few come in every day in their lunch break for something to do. Others come in because they're lonely; there are quite a few about. OAPs come in for a chat, have twenty minutes' browse; sometimes they buy but mostly they don't. We try to create a friendly atmosphere; people don't feel afraid to come in and we don't expect everyone to buy. Pensioners need cherishing. We put someone friendly on the till and have a toy-box for children.'
>
> (Manager Z, Oxford)

There is, however, a strong – if not universal – correlation between the formality of shop operations and procedures and levels of social interaction, with the most 'professionalised' outlets being least likely to generate a social network of regular customers who were welcomed regardless of purchase. Where consumers feel part of the shop's network, they can develop shop loyalty in terms of both consumption and donations, or may become involved as volunteers themselves, being drawn in further to the activities of the shop.

There are downsides to the development of more friendly relationships with customers, as they can monopolise sales assistants' time, pump the manager for information on the best purchases, and transfer an informal approach to their purchasing practices, pushing the boundaries on prices in particular: 'Most customers we know by first name start bargaining. It depends who they are; I say no if they're just trying it on' (Manager X, Oxford). However, personal knowledge of customers and their needs can serve both customers' interests and shop profits, especially if it generates return visits and subsequent purchases, as demonstrated by this manager: 'I know my customers and their wants and styles. I'll put things away for them before they've even seen them and point things out to people. I give friendly advice – try it on – give us a twirl.' This friendliness can have a commercial motivation: this manager continued, 'You have to waffle, it encourages them to buy' (Manager O, Oxford). It is in this area of customer service that charity shops can enhance their offering, giving time and attention to clients that they might not experience in other low-price shops. When this contributes to the building up of social relationships, there can be a significant impact on sales, as customers who feel welcome and valued return to become regular clients (Maddrell 2000).

What do people buy in charity shops?

The overwhelmingly dominant item purchased in charity shops is clothing and, more specifically, women's clothing, which might take up to three-quarters of floor space, reflecting the high proportion of women shoppers and volunteers (Parsons 2000) and the predominance of women's clothing in donated goods. This is in marked contrast to car boot fairs, where household goods and books dominate sales (Gregson and Crewe 1997a). In the Oxford sample, 69 per cent of women charity shoppers purchased clothes, marginally outstripped by men at 71 per cent. The highest proportion was to be found in the 18–30 age group, where in excess of 75 per cent of both women and men bought clothing. However, this is in marked contrast to the 31–40 age group, which had the lowest proportion of clothes buyers, both male and female: of these, only 25 per cent of men and 50 per cent of women charity shoppers bought clothes.

Items of children's clothing do go on to second and subsequent cycles of consumption, but, as noted in Chapter 4 on donations, these occur largely through private systems of exchange, whether by swapping or resale, making this a minor element within consumption patterns in charity shops, contrary to expectations. Despite these alternative networks for sale of second-hand children's clothes, this is an offering identified as an area of potential expansion by Mintel (1997), given the 17 per cent increase in expenditure on children's clothes nationally between 1996 and 2000. While it is a potential growth area, many charities will be reluctant to take this up, as experience to date shows that lower prices need to be charged per item compared to adult clothes, meaning there is less return per unit of rail space – it would take a significant increase in prices to match, let alone surpass, income from adult garments, unless a currently absent supply of high-quality children's clothes became available. Mintel (1997) suggests that one avenue for expansion could be selling *new* children's clothes, including quality seconds or fair trade clothing, through charity shops as a means of increasing turnover. However, the question remains as to whether it is possible to attract sufficient customers to shops not known for this type of offering and, more specifically, the type of consumers prepared to pay new-goods prices for these items.

It has been suggested that underwear, nightwear and shoes are often not sold in charity shops because of associations with bodily fluids, functions and hygiene (Gregson *et al.* 2000). This is widely (but not universally) true of underwear. Indeed, a 'give a bra' charity was set up in the UK in the 1990s to fill the supply gap for needy women, and charities that supply the local poor with second-hand clothing will raise funds to buy new underwear. For example, the Salvation Army in Oxford uses money raised from its charity shop for this purpose. However, normal boundaries of acceptance were shown to be negotiated by consumers when considering designer labels or collectable antique underwear (Gregson *et al.* 2000). Moreover, new packaged underwear is sold when donated, and managers of independent charity shops (e.g. local hospice shops) frequently sell second-hand underwear (as was noted in the Isle of Man, Liverpool and Oxford, for example). Again, while some of the large charity chains do not stock shoes and nightwear, the majority of charity shops do, despite associations with bodily 'pollution'. The widespread sale of swimwear also at least challenges the universality of the 'gusset' factor in the consumption of second-hand clothing, although it could be argued that swimwear's infrequency of wear or its wearing in water – particularly chlorinated water – might aid the psychological negotiation of its purchase and subsequent use.

In general terms, age appeared to have little impact on purchasing patterns, and Table 3.2 further illustrates a relative parity in terms of purchasing patterns by type of goods by men and women. The clear difference in purchasing patterns by gender is found in the case of fair trade goods, which were purchased by only 6 per cent of men (and only in the 18–30 age category) compared with 22 per cent of women. This gendered pattern was also reflected in Mintel's (1997) nationwide survey, which reported that 7 per cent of men and twice as many women bought fair trade goods. The 8 per cent differential in purchasing of household goods is also significant, with women buying more of these goods; books are purchased by a higher proportion of male charity shoppers (39 per cent) compared with female (29 per

Table 3.2 What people buy in charity shops by gender (Oxford)

Types of goods	Women (%)	Men (%)
Clothing	69	71
Children's clothing/toys	20	19
Books	29	39
Household items	24	16
New goods/gifts	22	16
Fair trade	22	6
Other		1[a]

Source: Maddrell (2000)

Note:
a Specifically CDs and other music products

cent). Interestingly, in the case of books, the converse pattern is seen in donations: a higher percentage of women donate books (see Chapter 4). There are examples of charity shops in rural areas offering library services within the shop, but more commonly charity shops act as a sort of 'pay as you read' club. Both men and women contribute to an ongoing series of consumption cycles of books (commonly 10–20 pence in non-specialist outlets (Parsons 2000)), consuming (reading) and then returning the books and/or others as donations. As one manager attested, 'It's like the little library corner here sometimes' (Manager P, Oxford). A variant of this type of recirculation of goods can occur with collectables: 'There's the stamp man. He buys thirty packs at £2.50 each, takes out what he wants and then returns the leftovers' (Manager J, Oxford).

As noted above, the increasing preoccupation with collecting categories of things is a characteristic of contemporary consumption, fuelled by television programmes and specialist magazines propounding the delights and potential financial gains of these activities, whether it be collections of watches, Star Wars toys and merchandise or Staffordshire pottery. Charity shops have been identified as a potential source of collectables both by individuals and by dealers hoping to find items of interest to sell on at profit. One manager (Manager V, Oxford) estimated that more than ten dealers or regular car-booters visited the shop each day, looking for items to sell on at profit. 'Dealers are always looking for particular things – books, bric-a-brac, designer labels – and ask you if you've got anything out back' (Manager I, Oxford). Being part of the informal market, these dealers often haggle over price and quantity in a way that is not welcomed by the majority of charity shops, and have been known to put other customers off goods they want to buy themselves:

'Some dealers try to knock the prices down. They're naughty, we're not here for them to knock us down then double the price.'
(Manager J, Oxford)

'They complain about prices more than local people. With records we use the *Musicmaker*'s pricing guide and then charge a bit cheaper – we want the profit [for the charity] not the dealer. One dealer deliberately put a customer off from buying a £65 camera, so we put it away and it wasn't on the shelf when the dealer came back.'
(Manager L, Oxford)

Dealers are able to profit from the ignorance of those running a charity shop when their specialist knowledge is greater than that of

Customers and demand 49

the shop staff. Charity shop managers attempt to address this problem by use of industry guides such as *Musicmaker* (mentioned above) or by engaging *ad hoc* or occasional specialist volunteers, such as jewellers or camera technicians, to value and repair goods for resale. Some dealers offer this service on the basis of 'first refusal' for things they look at, which seems to be very much to their advantage given the fact that they are advising on the value! However, there usually exists a problem of matching supply with demand to ensure the maximum income from a collectable donated item. Where centralised systems for collecting and recirculating donated goods are in place, these can be used in order to place collectables in specialist shops or in locations considered most likely to provide buyers. Large charities such as Oxfam are beginning to supersede this system by using their national Internet site as an auction place for collectables, thereby making known the availability of first-edition books or antiques or rare records to a potentially international market. This form of centralisation, specialisation and matching of goods to expertise is bound to be profitable and requires relatively small overheads. This must be a way forward for both large and small charities.

Specialisation and diversification

Despite original doubts about their viability, specialist charity bookshops are flourishing in suitable locations such as university towns, attracting academics, tourists, middle-class buyers and dealers – with a notably higher proportion of male consumers than general charity shops. Other specialist shops sell second-hand furniture (including Oxfam in Liverpool), retro fashion (shops in London and Manchester) or computers or other high-value goods that require specialist preparation (e.g. European Union-required safety checks on all electrical equipment for resale). Concentrating on these specialist offerings achieves a number of benefits for the charities. First, it allows the recruitment and targeting of specialist qualified staff, both voluntary and paid, who can contribute to the sorting, repairing/checking and pricing of donated goods as appropriate. As the manager of a specialist charity bookshop reported,

'We have one volunteer per area [type of book], so they know the market price, but they need a feel for selling, as well as specialised knowledge – what's collectable, first editions, good illustrators, signed copies, etc. It's often a lifetime's knowledge, but it also needs to be up to date.'

(Manager K, Oxford)

It may be easier for such specialist shops to attract qualified volunteers for a concentrated task – camera repair and valuation, for example – than it is for general charity shops needing a host of specialists on an irregular basis. Specialist outlets may also be successful in attracting specific appropriate donations (see Chapter 4). Additionally, they can improve their marketing and establish a reputation as a specialist outlet for what are usually comparative goods.

While specialisation has been identified as a key option for niche marketing, particularly by larger charity chains (see Phelan 1997 and Chapters 2 and 7), others are offering localised services as a diversification *within* an individual charity shop, commonly in rural areas. These services include house clearance or the disposal of bulky items as a development from bag collection, through to fancy dress hire and Post Office services. Other charity shops have developed links with other charity and service providers to provide community services such as acting as a locus for local mental health services, as in the case of the Mental Health (Scotland) Association (see Milligan 1999 and Chapter 5), representing an interactive reciprocal relationship between charity shops and their localities, other charities and state service providers.

Those who don't/won't

Although widely used, charity shops remain outside the boundaries of the universally acceptable or desirable arena of consumption, with almost a quarter of women and half of men never using them. Despite campaigns to lure potential shoppers, and in turn to retain their custom, this significant group of consumers has remained immune to the attractions of second-hand goods. These are not so much 'those who don't' as 'those who won't'. For many of those who choose not to purchase second-hand goods, it is this potential association of wearing someone else's clothes, along with the potential risk of dirt and disease which cannot be negotiated, which always acts as a barrier to buying second-hand clothing: 'Charity shop clothing, particularly adults' clothing, continues to be inscribed with death and disease, however "irrational" this might be. And consuming these clothes consequently remains construed as a risky practice' (Gregson *et al.* 2000: 117).

It is clear that a significant proportion of shoppers resist all sales of second-hand goods, particularly clothing, because of fear of previous owners – or fear of their traces of disease, death, sex and other bodily functions (Gregson *et al.* 2000). Older people who grew up surrounded by a greater threat of widespread infectious disease are inhibited by associations with illness; others, including parents, might fear the contamination of the young. Both are influenced (subconsciously) by the superstitious fear of association with death (ibid.). Even the purifying rituals of cleaning would not be sufficient to allow consumers to negotiate the 'various constructs of the body; the body as leaky excess; as polluting, contaminating, threatening, other; as material, subject to disease and death' (ibid.: 103). People have different attitudes to bodily functions, particularly those associated with sexual organs and sexual practice – hence the cry 'it all comes down to gussets' (ibid.: 111). However, as Gregson *et al.* recognise, these attitudes can change, as exemplified by the interviewee who started buying outer clothing such as coats and has gradually moved to buying items of clothing that are worn next to the skin. Generally accepting attitudes to babies' second-hand clothes – babies of course being notoriously leaky – serve to underline the role of sex in negotiating whether an item of clothing is saleable (on the part of volunteers and managers) and consumable (on the part of the shopper) (ibid.).

For some consumers the act of purchasing second-hand goods is perceived (in an often non-self-reflexive way) as a threat to their identity and self-image. It has been suggested that, secure in other forms of status, middle-class consumers are free to engage in second-hand consumption of some goods (e.g. clothes) in a way that would mark consumers from lower economic classes as social inferiors (see Gregson and Crewe 1997a, b, 1998 on car boot shoppers). Certainly, as Mintel's (1997) national survey suggests, up to 70 per cent of those in the poorest socio-economic group in the UK do not buy from charity shops, either by choice or by being excluded by higher prices in some charity shops. Some shoppers also argue that it is at best inappropriate, at worst immoral, for those with the purchasing ability to buy new goods to buy second-hand goods, thereby 'taking' from the disadvantaged: 'I don't need to [buy from charity shops] . . . I don't think it's right to buy things in charity shops if you can afford to buy from proper shops' (Shopper 21, Isle of Man).

Many men – and especially young men – appear to be particularly resistant to purchasing second-hand clothes, which is perhaps not surprising given the emphasis on branded status goods in mainstream contemporary male consumption discourses, and this group remains an untapped market for charity shops. Men under 50 years of age suggest that they would respond better to charity shop consumption sites if they had more new goods, better shop frontage and display, more sports goods and younger (more attractive) sales assistants

(Maddrell 2001a) – that is, if charity shops traded up further to become more like mainstream retailers.

The questions of why people shop in charity outlets and what they buy are central to understanding the market base and the role of charity shops in consumption culture, as well as aspects of their socio-economic functions for consumers. The continuum of types of charity shops suggested in Chapter 2 is overlain by a continuum of types of consumer using charity shops in different ways, including restriction to particular types of outlet and seasonal consumption, those immersed in second and subsequent cycle consumption and those positively avoiding these goods. Some of these complexities can be seen in the consumption of new goods retailed by charities.

In many ways the sale of new goods is both a form of specialisation and a means of negotiating many of the negative perceptions associated with charity shops and their products. New goods arguably encourage a different form of consumption, one that is less to do with combining charity and thrift and more to do with combining charity with the purchase of (generally) higher-quality products and associated lifestyle statements. Predominantly associated with second-hand items, bought-in goods represent an opportunity for extending the range and quality of goods offered to existing clientele but also for attracting a different type of consumer to charity shops. Those shopping in National Trust or RSPB (Royal Society for the Protection of Birds) shops generally do not perceive themselves as shopping in a charity shop as such, although they may have a sense of 'supporting charity'. Yet these are indeed charity shops, simply retailing 100 per cent bought-in new goods in a formal retailing context and generally attracting more people from the higher socio-economic groups (A, B and C) than charity shops offering predominantly second-hand goods – including those who would not consider buying from a typical charity shop for the reasons discussed above. Within the wider charity shop sector, bought-in-new (BIN) goods are associated with Oxfam, Barnardo's, the Imperial Cancer Research Fund and Save the Children (and accounting for 15 per cent, 13 per cent, 18 per cent and 27 per cent of their sales respectively in 2000 (Goodall 2000b)). While BIN goods are seen as an opportunity to increase turnover and profits (particularly given difficulties with donated stock) (Goodall 2000b), the fact that these would generally be sold alongside second-hand goods does little to mitigate the fears of those who 'won't' shop in charity shops. The larger charity chains offering new goods alongside second-hand items have negotiated this problem in various ways. Their strategies include separation of the use space of the locale of the shop, placing new goods at the very front of the shop between the window, entrance and till, allowing shoppers to avoid (the contamination of) second-hand goods should they wish to do so, as well as devoting window display to new goods. Also, more floor space is devoted to new goods at times of seasonal demand, such as Christmas. At these times, second-hand goods may be relegated to another room or floor of the shop, which can allow the matching of supply to demand for giftware. It can also help give the appearance of a shop that reflects the image of other mainstream competitors, thereby potentially allowing those consumers who 'won't' use charity shops to cross the shop boundary, without offending their sensibilities or transgressing their criteria for gifts.

However, the sale of BIN goods can exclude those for whom the new goods are less desirable: 'I'm not really interested in new goods, so I'm less interested in Oxfam now [since their introduction of BIN goods]. They're not really the things I thought they were there for – and they're too expensive' (shopper, female 31- to 40-year-old artist/ researcher, Liverpool).

Charity catalogues and Internet sales

A related form of consumption is through charity catalogues and the emerging area of Internet sales. The latter has the advantage of relatively low-cost dissemination, but it also relies primarily upon being sought out by potential consumers with Internet access and credit cards. Despite these limitations, charity e-commerce is growing in North America, with charities either selling direct on the Internet or using charity-shopper sites either to promote their merchandise or get donations or rebates/commission from sales on for-profit online shopping sites – for example, Charitymall.com and Shop2give.com (see Grobman 2000). Internet sales clearly represents an area for charities to consider for expansion and could reach those who resist high street charity shops – especially the large number of male Internet users (see Chapter 7). Charity catalogues (often seasonal) are widely circulated by mailshot to both those affiliated to a charity (e.g. Amnesty International members) or more generally (e.g. Save the Children), giving the potential for a wide readership. Use of these catalogues by Oxford shoppers would appear to mirror wider patterns of charity consumption, being used by 22 per cent of respondents, two-thirds of these users being women (Maddrell 2001a). This in part reflects the gendered character of wider shopping practices, illustrated in the several male respondents who knew that the catalogues were used within the household 'but my wife does it'. Almost two-thirds of users were those in C1 and C2 occupations, with pensioners accounting for a further 20 per cent. Only 10 per cent were in A or B professions, and 5 per cent were unemployed.

However, there are regional discrepancies, with almost 50 per cent of shoppers surveyed in the Isle of Man using charity catalogues (in part reflecting relatively high use of mail order shopping on the island). While some of these consumers were random in their use of these catalogues (including those who couldn't name the charity), the majority were committed to channelling their consumption by supporting one or more charity, suggesting greater brand loyalty to charity catalogues than to charity shops. Where more than one charity catalogue was used, the charities were usually cognate – for example, the 31- to 40-year-old professional woman who shopped from both Oxfam and Traidcraft catalogues and the 40-year-old male chef who bought from the Royal Society for the Protection of Birds (RSPB) and the Wildfowl and Wetland Trust (WWT).

The image of catalogue sales as a means for the lower classes to buy (lower-quality) goods, often by hire purchase, has been revolutionised in recent years with the growth of mail order consumption, particularly amongst the middle classes, seen in the advent of Next and even Harrods catalogues. Catalogue and Internet sales are an area of predicted growth within retailing generally and are almost certain to grow as a means of charity retailing – the fact that 40 per cent of non-users of charity shops in the Isle of Man did use charity catalogues, for example, suggests that there are at least regional markets where charity retailing can be expanded to reach current non-patrons. This view is reinforced if one considers the number of non-users who cite new, higher-quality goods and designer labels as the offerings that would make them consider shopping in charity outlets. Use of mail order or e-commerce allows shoppers to combine their consumption with supporting charity from the comfort of their home or without the necessity of leaving their workplace – and without having to cross the threshold of a charity shop. With the right offering this may prove to be particularly appealing to the 18–40 years age group, especially those men who may not generally experience consumption as a social activity.

4 Materialising profit
Donation and distribution

The vast majority of charity shops rely on donated goods for the bulk if not totality of their retail offering. Even chains such as Oxfam and the Save the Children Fund, known for their new goods, generated 85 per cent and 73 per cent of profits respectively from donated goods in 2000 (Goodall 2000a). This concentration on the sale of donated goods is also legally and fiscally significant as it affects the tax status of the shop operations. For example, as mentioned in Chapter 2, the sale of donated goods is currently free of VAT in the UK, as the transaction is considered to be 'realisation of a gift' rather than a sale (Horne and Broadbridge 1995). Charity shops compete with one another for second-hand goods as the sector has grown arguably to saturation point. They also face competition from private for-profit opportunities for resale of second-hand goods, including car boot, table top and garage sales, 'Nearly New' and 50/50 shops (known as Consignment shops in the USA), as these opportunities combine with the general public's awareness of the increased value of second-hand goods (Benaday 1997). The result is that people are donating less to charities (Mintel 1997).

In the face of this increased competition between the growing number of charity shops in the 1990s, particularly those opened on the basis of a centralised marketing decision rather than a specific local support or interest group, many charities have found themselves short of donated stock. The *NGO Finance* report survey identified shortage of stock as a key concern of charity respondents: 18 per cent in 1999 (Phelan 1999b) and 11 per cent in 2000 (Goodall 2000b) (the apparent decline may not represent an actual decline in the problem; it could merely mean that other worries have surfaced such as the collapse in the rag market in 1999–2000).

In mainstream retailing, location is always said to be the critical success factor: the location takes precedence over merchandise because even if the merchandise is just right, if the location is wrong the venture will fail. In charity retailing the constant pressure, for those selling mainly donated goods, is for stock acquisition. This chapter gives an insight into how charity shops attract and maintain donations of stock and what happens to goods on their entry into a new stage in their multiple cycles of consumption.

Physical distribution is basically concerned with product availability – that is, getting the right product to the right place at the right time (Howe 1992). It is the handling and movement of goods in order to provide a level of service that will satisfy customers. When we are dealing with the unknown quantity and quality of donated goods, the importance of selecting an appropriate distribution channel is crucial. These channels are a strategic asset that can lead to a sustainable competitive advantage (Dalrymple and Parsons 1995).

The historic method of goods acquisition by charity shops has been by means of the donor delivering goods to a specific shop. The donor is unknown and is thanked by the staff member receiving the goods, but no information is gleaned about the donor, or indeed about the nature of the goods donated. This method is still widely used across the sector but has engendered problems. In the mid-1980s, with the pedestrianisation of many UK town centres, driving and parking outside the shop in order to drop off a quantity of goods was rendered difficult or impossible. The effort required on the part of the donor was thereby increased, and consequently there was a drop in the quantity of donated goods; convenience of disposal of unwanted goods is a significant factor influencing donation behaviour.

Ease of delivery of donations is a recurring theme for many charity shop managers. For example, all the managers with charity shops located in the pedestrian zone in Hereford specifically attributed the lack of donations to the lack of vehicular access. As one Liverpool manager reported, 'The yellow lines are a real problem, there's a problem with parking, especially with the traffic wardens around here. Oxfam and Barnardo's are okay [with parking nearby], they get more donations than we do' (Manager G, Liverpool). Similarly, charity shops located in largely non-residential city centre locations can lack donations: 'We don't get very much brought in direct, we rely on a van collection across the region' (Manager T, Oxford); 'We rely almost entirely on the depot for clothes; people don't come into town with donations' (Manager J, Oxford). Clearly, the desire to locate charity outlets in areas of high footfall and hence the trend towards locating in central high street areas may benefit potential sales, but is not necessarily helpful with regard to the supply of second-hand goods where local donations are relied upon for the bulk of stock. However, the supply of goods is less crucial where the majority of stock is supplied centrally from warehouses, as is increasingly the case for the larger, more professionalised chains of charity shops.

The main method used by charities to combat difficulties with donor deliveries to the charity shop was that of the bag drop, now a familiar part of door-to-door delivery – a plastic bag left with a household and a date given for collection by the charity concerned. Although all charities welcome donations through the door of a charity shop, most have adopted the bag drop in order to have some proactive control over giving. The larger charities began bag drop operations in the late 1980s, with smaller and newer chains embarking on them later. Charities interviewed in Scotland, when asked about switching to bag drops, suggested that 'Donations through the door are a diminishing resource' and 'we used to rely on through-the-door donations, but due to an increase in pressure now we have to collect ourselves'; 'the principal and proactive way of procuring stock is by doing bag drops'; 'house-to-house collections are now of paramount importance' (Manager 3, Stirling).

Those involved with bag collections of donations on a regular basis get to know the amount and quality of goods likely to be obtained in a particular residential area. Such information might, in complex collection systems, be formally logged, or simply become a piece of expert knowledge on the part of the collector:

'The lower working class owner-occupied houses are the best [for bag donations], they give all the labels. The smart larger houses in north Oxford give rubbish; it's been good quality, but it's smelling like mad from being worn in the garden and it's full of holes – they've never had to shop in a charity shop, so they have no idea what to expect. The nouveau riche who give, give very generously and it's never dirty'.

(Manager Q, Oxford)

On a location note, it is interesting to contrast the experience of this bag collection on behalf of a shop from outside the immediate locality with the experience of a manager running a charity shop actually in north Oxford, who acknowledged the 'unusually good support when others seem to struggle. . . . We get all of our stuff over the door, except for a small supplement from the warehouse' (Manager N, Oxford). This suggests a further complexity to donation patterns, reflecting the relationship between location, socio-economic status of residents and donations to local shops as distinct from bag collections for a shop located elsewhere.

Targeting potential donors in their homes increases the charity's potential to control merchandising: 'Monitoring our sales affects our distribution – we can look at what is being sold and then see what we must stock to meet the customer need, then we can look at the best way to acquire this stock' (Manager 4, Stirling). Bag collections usually involve leaving a professionally printed collection bag with the charity's logo and a leaflet giving instructions regarding what to place in the bag and when to leave it out for collection, as well as information about the charity intended to encourage interest in and identification with that particular charity.

As with the shops themselves, the donation bags serve as an opportunity to promote the mission of the charity. Bags are collected and delivered to the commissioning shop or cluster from the charity chain or taken to a central warehouse if appropriate. Both individual shops and collection warehouses can operate to a systematic calendar and systematic geographical coverage, or respond to a specific shortfall in donated goods. This collection work is done by a variety of personnel, depending on the charity. Door-to-door collection by central warehouses is often done by full- or part-time paid drivers. Individual shops use part-time paid drivers (for example, *ad hoc* employment of house clearance specialists), or volunteers, including community service workers and *ad hoc* volunteers (usually men, often partners of regular volunteers), or even (in small, relatively unsupported operations) rely upon the managers themselves: 'I started doing van-drops [of collection bags] – we got a brilliant response; I go with the assistant manager to collect. We do car boot sales for the shop on a Sunday too, on a voluntary basis' (Manager X, Oxford).

Despite the occasional involvement of female managers and volunteers, bag collection is commonly designated as 'heavy work' and as such is commonly a gendered task reserved for men.

When goods are dropped at the shop door the donor pays for all distribution costs. The introduction of bag drops resulted in substantial costs to the charity, which have to be covered by continuing to attract good-quality goods for sale. This extra expense pushes the shop up the retail cycle (see Chapter 2) and thus into a more professional operation. The costs incurred by bag drops include the transport (either purchased or leased), fuel, and the labour costs of the driver as well as the cost of the bags themselves.

Of sixteen charities interviewed in Scotland, two had no idea how much the bag drops were costing them but used the system because 'everyone else was'. Others suggested: 'It is very expensive, but we can reduce costs by using volunteers and recycling bags' and 'The costs are quite substantial – for example, bags alone cost £70–£100 per 1,000' (Manager C, Scotland). However, the effectiveness of the bag drop is not in doubt. To quote various charity shop managers, 'I don't believe that bag drops are cost-effective – I know they are'; 'The cost is worth it when the density of stock improves, which in turn increases sales'; 'For every £1 spent £4.50 comes back as sales proceeds'; 'If it wasn't cost-effective we wouldn't be doing it'; 'There is a very good cost to profit ratio'.

Charity shops have different mechanisms for evaluating the profitability of bag drops, relative to costs. These include monitoring sales after input from bag drops, or more sophisticated accounting systems allowing managers to differentiate income from direct donations and bag-drop donations, allowing the profitability of bag drops to be monitored. However, others have few effective means of quantifying income derived: 'We know the volume of stock from house-to-house collection but we don't know how many sales are from these' (Scottish retail director).

Warehousing and bag collections

Shortage of donated goods in the late 1980s and 1990s motivated greater local and regional and even inter-regional co-ordination of stock between shops within a charity chain. This echoes the central management of goods achieved in formal retailing chains through electronic point of sales (EPOS) systems, but is achieved in a variety of ways within the charity sector, with varying degrees of formality and technicality. Some charities continue to rely on over-the-door donations but operate a transfer system whereby information about surpluses and shortages can be logged centrally. Van drivers are then dispatched to move surpluses to areas of shortage, often on the basis of labelled or colour-coded bags (e.g. red for women's dresses, brown for men's clothes). Alternatively, in addition to local door-to-door collection of donated goods from residential areas in bags bearing the charity's logo, some large charities operate regional sweeps of residential areas over several counties in a relatively sophisticated response to seasonal and locational demand. These goods are then collected, sorted, cleaned and stored, and in some cases priced, in a central warehouse before being dispatched to the relevant charity shops. Items are also commonly given a code indicating the first week of display on the shop floor, allowing the identification of goods to be withdrawn for recirculation to other shops or for price reduction within the shop after a given period (typically two to four weeks), depending on shop and/or chain policy.

By the end of the 1990s the large charity shop chains in the UK were all operating formal warehousing systems. At least nine charities were operating or seriously considering a formal warehouse distribution system. 'We are trying to get the right goods in the right place at the right time – meeting customer needs is an issue and a depot and distribution system idea helps us with this' (UK retail director).

Charity retailers are feeling intense competition in their sector (Phelan 1996), and to overcome this they are rethinking their strategies for attracting and holding customers. Without the right stock in the right place at the right time, charity retailers, like all retailers, are unable to satisfy the needs of their customers. They have to rethink their stock generation and distribution strategies in order to overcome the problem. While not a silver bullet solution, the bag drop does offer a degree of control to the charity retailer, in addition to being a cost-effective alternative to falling, over-the-door donations: 'Control is a big issue and bag drops do increase control'; 'The quantity of stock is controlled this way and in turn the shops can be more selective about what they sell'; 'It offers control over the stock moving through stores'; 'There is more control over timing when goods come into the store, which means stock flow can be regulated' (UK retail director).

Centralised management and control has become an issue, and a bag-drop system that is co-ordinated and operated under national guidelines is an effective way to organise a distribution system. The majority of charity shops carry out sales monitoring and in this way customer needs are identified. Charity retailers are examining the possibility of implementing more new, refined systems of warehouses and formal distribution networks in order to extend their competitive advantage and focus further on meeting their customers' needs.

Some charities, such as Oxfam, operate a formal supply chain based on circulating a specific number of items of clothing between shops on a fortnightly basis, providing, for example, 200 items of clothing to be moved to the next shop in the chain while receiving 200 new items themselves. In some chains this applies only to the main offering, namely women's clothes. Shops can be organised in priority order, with a high-performance shop (in terms of price and/or turnover) receiving the highest-quality goods at the 'top' of the circulation chain, with unsold goods ultimately reaching a discount shop, usually in a more socio-economically deprived area, such as Oxfam Supersaver (discount) shops, or going to a Wastesaver recycling centre, or being collected for ragging. Centralised processing or co-ordination of donated goods can assist in matching supply and demand of particular products. The separating out of specialist items such as collectables, books or retro fashion means that they can be sold in the location where demand will ensure that the highest price will be achieved. For example, evening suits, ball gowns and party dresses collected regionally are sold centrally to students in Oxford around the time of May Balls or in the Morningside area of Edinburgh. Warehouse-based sorting operations can refine such targeting further, with certain items being designated for another part of the country or even to be sold abroad.

These systems ensure both that individual charity shops are not dependent upon local donations in order to trade, and that there is a variety of stock. This system can also deliver seasonally appropriate stock, as this can be stored in bulk in a warehouse on a scale impossible for individual shops, which are often short of back-room space. However, these systems are not met with unqualified approval within individual outlets:

> 'The stock rotation is a good system, but it's a moot point with some people. The system varies; I may [be told] to move on 300 items, but the next shop only wants 170, or the previous one sends on 450 . . . it does allow me to send out-of-season stuff back to the warehouse. Seasonal changes always start with initial stock from [the warehouse]. We've resisted exchange between shops; we only do it if we're desperate, when we'll get stuff from Wales or Reading.'
>
> (Manager M, Oxford)

Charity shops use a combination of methods, therefore, in order to generate their stock. Volunteers and managers are loci for donations. They bring their own contributions (98 per cent of volunteers donate goods; see Chapter 5), but, more significantly in terms of quantity, also attract donations from friendship and kin networks, as well as directly and indirectly soliciting donations from customers in the shop as staff get to know regular shoppers: 'The customers have got to know me and bring things in' (Manager Q, Oxford).

Many charity shops benefit from a small but steady supply of donations from neighbouring retailers or businesses. While not repudiating all tension between competitive formal retailers and charity shops, this co-operation contrasts markedly with the media image of discord between the two. City centre charity outlets benefit from larger (non-competitive) stores:

'[A small department store] gives us new goods, which is great for our bric-a-brac. [A large department store] give us unsold stock, also lost property that hasn't been claimed, like umbrellas. The bookshop gives us quite a lot too.'

(Manager J, Oxford)

Specialist charity shops, too, can benefit from related business donations. Charity bookshops, for example, may receive donations from other bookshops and local publishers, as well as members of the general public who are aware both that marginal-interest books will sell and that higher prices are achieved in the specialist shop. This suggests a further advantage in niche marketing, namely that of benefiting from 'niche donations', as well as the potential to match volunteer interest and expertise to the shop's activity.

We have now explored the problem of merchandising from the perspective of the charity retailer, but what do we know of the donors who give items to be sold? Understanding householders' responses to these requests for donations is seen by some charities as vital to the continued supply of second-hand goods. The main area of research in which the issue of consumer disposal behaviour is treated relates to environmentalism and the green consumer (e.g. Lord and Putrevu 1998). Of the few studies of disposal that have been carried out outside the domain of the green consumer, the main focus has been on the role goods carry as conveyors of meaning and identity (McCracken 1990; Campbell 1986), and the process of disposal is described as a means of identity maintenance or change. For example, Young (1991) explored consumer dispositions during life transitions and found that individuals discarded goods as a means of shedding aspects of their identity that they no longer valued or wished to emphasise. More recently, Curasi *et al.* (1998) examined the disposal of goods by older consumers and found that dispensing with valued possessions was an important process in transferring meaning to family and friends.

Both lines of research on consumer disposal outlined above provide some insights into how consumers manage the turnover of goods that feature in their lives, but there remains a dearth of research indicating how used-goods markets are supplied. Horne and Hibbert (2001) surveyed 210 households in three different housing areas in Scotland in order to gather descriptive data on individuals' disposal behaviour. They determined that in the space of a year the greatest proportions of goods disposed of were women's (93 per cent) and men's (78 per cent) clothing, followed by books (62 per cent) and furniture (50 per cent). Thirty-eight per cent of the sample reported disposing of toys and children's clothes, although this represents virtually 100 per cent of households with children in them. Respondents were least likely to have disposed of music products on records, CDs and tapes (17 per cent). 'Other' categories of goods disposed of included white goods, soft furnishings, ornaments, crockery and cutlery.

Table 4.1 details the channels through which individuals disposed of different types of goods. The first figure in each cell represents the number of respondents who had disposed of a particular type of good through a particular channel. The two numbers in *italics* are the column and row percentages respectively. The figure in parentheses underneath the row totals is the proportion of goods disposed of through that channel, as a percentage of the total number of goods discarded through all channels.

From Table 4.1 it can be seen that 50 per cent of goods were given to charity, 17 per cent were given to family, and friends, and just 13 per cent were thrown away. The jumble sale, a traditional fund-raising medium for, usually, a local-based charity, cause or church, was the fourth most used method of disposal. The three disposal routes for self-gain, 'sold at a car boot sale', 'sold through a newspaper' and 'sold through a second-hand shop', were used for the disposal of a relatively small proportion of goods (4 per cent, 4 per cent and 3 per cent respectively). Other methods of disposal suggested by respondents referred to items given to one-off fund-raising events or hospitals.

Table 4.1 reveals the pattern of disposal for different types of goods. For example, the majority of books (42.5 per cent) are given to charity, although usage of this channel of disposal is relatively low when compared to the average for other categories of goods. In contrast, books are more often given to family and friends or to jumble sales than other types of goods. It is relatively rare for books to be thrown away; only 6.5 per cent were disposed of in this way compared to 13 per cent of all types of goods. If books are sold for personal gain, it is through car boot sales (5 per cent). Records, CDs and tapes are similarly donated to charity and given to family and friends, although a larger percentage of these are thrown away (23.6 per cent) or sold for personal gain. Children's toys follow a similar pattern of being given to charity and family and friends. Jumble sales are more widely used to dispose of toys than any other category of good and, compared to the average for all types of goods, there is a relatively low incidence of toys being thrown away (Horne and Hibbert 2001).

There are similarities between the patterns of disposal for men's and women's clothes, but some marked differences for children's

Table 4.1 Ways in which consumers dispose of different types of used goods

	Books	Records/CDs/tapes	Toys	Women's clothes	Men's clothes	Children's clothes	Furniture	Other	Row totals
Given to jumble sale	31 / 15.5 / 35.2	4 / 7.3 / 4.5	20 / 16.9 / 22.7	11 / 4.0 / 12.5	8 / 3.6 / 9.1	6 / 4.5 / 6.8	3 / 2.1 / 3.4	5 / 9.6 / 5.7	88 (7.4)
Sold at car boot sale (for self)	10 / 5.0 / 21.2	4 / 7.3 / 8.5	9 / 7.6 / 19.1	7 / 2.6 / 14.9	5 / 2.3 / 10.6	6 / 4.5 / 12.8	1 / 0.7 / 2.1	5 / 9.6 / 10.6	47 (3.9)
Given to charity	85 / 42.5 / 14.3	18 / 32.7 / 3.0	48 / 40.7 / 8.1	171 / 62.9 / 28.8	145 / 65.9 / 24.4	68 / 51.1 / 11.4	43 / 29.7 / 7.2	16 / 30.7 / 2.7	594 (49.7)
Sold through a newspaper	3 / 1.5 / 6.4	6 / 10.9 / 12.8	4 / 3.4 / 8.5	6 / 2.2 / 12.8	6 / 2.7 / 12.8	7 / 5.3 / 14.9	9 / 6.2 / 19.1	6 / 11.5 / 12.8	47 (3.9)
Sold through second-hand shop	4 / 2.0 / 14.8	2 / 3.6 / 7.4	0 / 0.0 / 0.0	10 / 3.7 / 37.0	4 / 1.8 / 14.8	1 / 0.8 / 3.7	4 / 2.8 / 14.8	2 / 3.8 / 7.4	27 (2.3)
Given to friends/family	47 / 23.5 / 22.5	11 / 20 / 5.3	24 / 20.3 / 11.5	28 / 10.3 / 13.4	18 / 8.2 / 8.6	29 / 21.8 / 13.9	43 / 29.7 / 20.6	9 / 17.3 / 4.3	209 (17.5)
Thrown away	13 / 6.5 / 8.6	9 / 16.4 / 6.0	9 / 7.6 / 6.0	35 / 12.9 / 23.2	29 / 13.2 / 19.2	11 / 8.3 / 7.3	38 / 26.2 / 25.2	7 / 13.4 / 4.6	151 (12.6)
Other	7 / 3.5 / 21.9	1 / 1.8 / 3.1	4 / 3.4 / 12.5	4 / 1.5 / 12.5	5 / 2.3 / 15.6	5 / 3.8 / 15.6	4 / 2.8 / 12.5	2 / 3.8 / 6.3	32 (2.7)
Column totals	200	55	118	272	220	133	145	52	1,195

Source: Horne and Hibbert (2001)

Note: See text for an explanation of what the figures represent.

clothes. A high percentage of men's and women's clothes are given to charity, whereas the proportion of children's clothes disposed of through this channel is comparable to the average for all goods. The next most common method of disposal for adult clothes is to throw them away, whereas this is relatively uncommon for children's clothes, which tend to be passed on to family and friends, as has been found in a number of studies. Sixty-nine per cent of donors in Oxford gave clothing (very similar to the proportion buying clothing); children's things, books and household goods were each donated by approximately one-quarter of donors, and new goods by 12 per cent (Maddrell 2001a). A quarter of Oxford donors may give children's clothes or toys, but generally charity shops are short of children's clothes, owing to a lack of donations that is largely attributable to the existence of alternative forms of informal recirculation, and to repeated consumption cycles that eventually make the clothes unsaleable. Such repeated consumption occurs most obviously with hand-me-downs within nuclear or extended families or friendship groups or networks, such as toddler groups or lesbian mothers' groups. Children's clothes (as well as toys, equipment, etc.) also represent a major offering at events such as regular parent and toddler group sales (see Clarke 2000 on the Lonsdale Mothers' Group). As one Oxford manager reported, 'Once I got to know mums here, I realised that most of the kids' clothes were exchanged by swaps. I stopped trying to [sell] them and just keep a small children's rail' (Manager O, Oxford).

Finally, the disposal of furniture follows a quite different pattern. Most disposal of furniture is split among charities, family and friends and items being thrown away. There is far less use of charities as a channel of disposal for furniture than for other types of goods, and a far greater incidence of giving items to family and friends or throwing them out. Charities need to have specialist outlets (and collection systems) or sufficient flexible-use shop floor space to be able to accommodate bulky items – for example, where rents are low. However, furniture represents a form of specialisation some charities are moving into, especially where house clearance can be offered. Types of goods donated in Oxford ranged from clothing to bedding and trinkets. In the absence of a specialist furniture charity shop in Oxford, nobody donated furniture, unlike in Liverpool, which has a large Oxfam furniture shop stocked with donated goods (Maddrell 2001a).

In terms of general motives for donating goods, supporting charity (either specific or generalised) was the main factor, influencing 79 per cent of Oxford donors; 48 per cent were influenced by the opportunity for convenient disposal and 37 per cent by the desire to recycle goods. In terms of gender, just over half of women and men wanted to support charity through their donated goods (58 per cent and 52 per cent respectively), but almost half (43 per cent) of men were also influenced by the opportunity for convenient disposal, compared to just over a quarter (27 per cent) of women. Recycling was the least influential factor, confined to the under 50 years age groups and most influencing women between 31 and 40 years of age (58 per cent) (Maddrell 2001a). This could suggest that environmental concern is less influential on the world-view and lifestyle of older people and more influential for women in the age group most associated in contemporary British society with child rearing.

So, while offering the ultimate convenience for donating goods (a significant factor for donors as identified in the Oxford study), response to door-to-door collection is made more complex by a number of factors. These include charity loyalty, frequency of collections by any given and competing charities, and the time of year, with shops benefiting from seasonal clearouts, for example: 'It was brilliant today, everyone must have had a mass clear-out over Easter' (Manager M, Oxford).

Attitude to material goods is also a significant factor in donation patterns. For example, individuals with a relatively minimalist approach who possess only those items they wish to keep will have little to pass on, whereas others who have goods to spare may still place a personal value on those items and want them to 'get the best price'. This 'best price' is in part for the charity, but also as a reflection of the value they place on their belongings and therefore their class status or broader identity. This latter factor was identified as a pricing issue with volunteers, who commonly over-priced their own donations (see Maddrell 2000 and Chapter 5).

Many charity shop users also donate goods to the shops. This has implications for the chain of consumption, as patrons of charity shops who both donate and purchase goods are involved with both the 'production' and the consumption of goods, echoing the 'fluidity of modes of participation' by buyers and sellers at car boot fairs (Gregson and Crewe 1997a). One major charity retailer claims that almost two-thirds of its customers have donated goods to the shops at some stage in the past. The donors were most prevalent from the AB social class, from those working part-time and from those in the 55- to 64-year age group. This retailer also suggests that a higher percentage of the donating customers shopped at the 'older-style' shops rather than the new, refurbished stores (UK retail director).

As with many aspects of participation in consumption via charity shops, gender is a significant factor in donation patterns. For example, in Oxford 42 per cent of male consumers in charity shops did *not* donate goods, compared with a much smaller proportion of female consumers (13 per cent) (Maddrell 2001a). However, this gender distinction is cross-cut by age as these non-donors were drawn predominantly from the 18–30 years age group in the case of women, as were a significant number of the non-donating men. In total, 65 per cent of men and women in the 18–30 age group do not donate to charity shops, leading us to conclude that young people, particularly young men, are less likely to be donors of goods to charity shops (Maddrell 2001a).

The only clear gender distinction in donation patterns for specific goods was in the case of books, where 38 per cent of women donated books, compared to 25 per cent of men (this being the inverse of the gendered purchasing pattern of books in charity shops in Oxford; see Chapter 3). Two characteristics of donation patterns by age can be seen in relation to gifts of clothing: all women in the 31–40 age group donated clothes (this being the age group least likely to buy clothes in a charity shop – about 50 per cent), and men over 60 years of age donate only clothes. However, it is important to note that the very unpredictability of donations results in the eclectic stock that is the source of pleasure for many who shop in charity shops (as well as other second-hand markets) (Parsons 1996).

Local charities with a high profile often attract a large proportion of locally donated goods (e.g. local hospices, or Oxfam in its home town of Oxford). However, localised and individualised responses by donors when asked about donation disposition suggest three factors: first, that specific charities attract specific donors (e.g. those with some personal link with the charity – as is the case with some volunteers; see Chapter 5); second, that proximity can create a degree of identification with a particular shop or charity, and/or facilitate donations; and third, that overall, people seem to have a higher degree of charity loyalty when it comes to donations as compared with consumption patterns. One donor declared, 'I always bring my things here' (donor, shop H, Liverpool). This higher degree of loyalty to cause/shop in donation of goods than in consumption of charity shop goods is a general phenomenon. Loyalty in donations is particularly common where donors have a personal association with the shop, staff or charity itself, for example if a relative has suffered from a disease relevant to the charity or has benefited from a local service. Such loyalty can be seen particularly in the case of independent charity shops raising funds for a local charity, notably hospice shops, whereby donations become part of the dialectical relationship between the patient and their family as supporters of and beneficiaries from the charity. The relationship can continue after the death of the patient when homes are cleared and goods are donated to the hospice shop, often in addition to formal bequests. As in the case of volunteering to help in charity shops, these types of donations can be therapeutic and seen as a positive element of the grieving process. They can be seen not merely as a convenient but as a *positive* disposal of the deceased's material goods, even an opportunity to reinscribe the meaning of those goods from inalienable and therefore indisposable (because of the personal association) to alienable and disposable because the goods continue their 'social life' via an avenue approved by the deceased (Appadurai 1988). This ritual process of divestment (McCracken 1988) (like the giving of *any* item into the second-hand market) may involve the removal of personal items and identifiers such as brooches, badges or name labels and cleaning the item.

Leading on from this idea of 'ritual divestment', whether sourced from door-to-door collection or delivered over the door, is the fact that donated items need to be sorted, cleaned and priced before being presented on the shop floor. This initial work is considered to be relatively 'heavy' work and is commonly undertaken by volunteers, particularly those who for various reasons prefer to avoid front-of-shop work (see Chapter 5). The initial sorting usually involves the opening of bags and categorising items into type, such as men's and women's clothing, toys, etc., as well as items that are deemed unsaleable, which might be allocated for sale to rag merchants in the case of clothing or household linen or for disposal as rubbish in the case of soiled or broken items. Charity shop managers report rejecting up to 80 per cent of donated goods because of poor quality (including soiled goods). Charity shops retailing in economically advantaged areas maintain particularly high standards in keeping with class expectations. 'We get the best-quality goods. Marks and Spencer is the lowest label we sell; we've got a Vivienne Westwood suit' (Manager J, Oxford). In contrast, for charities with a mission to serve local needy people, there is an added aspect of sorting goods suitable for the use of their clientele, as is the case for the Salvation Army, which collects clothing and household goods for the very poor, homeless or asylum seekers.

Some volunteers refuse to do sorting because this operation is most associated with the worst aspects of second-hand goods: smell, dirt, disease and death.

'The bags can be a health and safety issue; you can't refuse them, but you don't know what's in them. You can get anything in the bags, we've had used condoms and leftovers from the Sunday roast. Sometimes we get what we call "dead bags", after someone has died and the things are all stained with bodily fluids.'

(Assistant Manager H, Liverpool)

'Some [bags] are very good, some are absolutely filthy – especially when the students go home – [the content] mostly goes to rags.'

(Manager T, Oxford)

The cleaning and re-presenting of donated goods is a significant stage in the biography of an item offered for resale in a charity shop and merits further attention in the emerging literature on charity shops. This process is significant because it is often one of transformation, as an item emerges in the back room of the charity shop or warehouse sorting area from mixed bags of donations, and will eventually be sold for £5.95, realising a significant profit for the charity. The same item would have a negligible rag value (determined by weight) or might fetch 10p at a jumble sale. As Gregson *et al.* (2000) point out, second-hand goods make us critically aware of the differences between commodities, notably the role of the item's previous history (especially bodily associations) and those items that have (an often related) resale value or not, the value being increased by the cleaning. This is the stage at which charity shop assistants, usually female volunteers, make a major contribution to the charity in adding to the value of the product through their labour. Lury (1999) notes how women, while being primary consumers in Euro-American society, are also producers because of their further work on purchased goods prior to their consumption in the household. This can be seen most obviously in the case of food, but also in the production of clothes and furnishings from purchased fabric, for example. In the same way, voluntary labour partially 'produces' donated goods for resale in charity shops through making goods clean and attractive to potential buyers.

Early charity shops washed and ironed any donated clothes that arrived at the shop in an unpresentable state, but this is time- and labour-intensive and usually beyond the facilities of the shop, meaning it was something that had to be done by volunteers or shop managers at home. Charity shops have increasingly moved to steam cleaners (widely used in formal retailing to remove transit creases in goods) as these can be hand operated, take relatively little storage space and remove surface dirt as well as creases, making ironing unnecessary.

These machines do not clean as thoroughly as immersion washing, but clothing from charity shops is rarely worn without washing, the act of washing or dry-cleaning being an important part of the consumer's divestment of the previous owner and their bodily fluids (Gregson *et al.* 2000). The washing of clothes by immersion also has connotations of baptism: rejection of the past, renewal, new life and identity.

5 Staffing the charity shop

Voluntary, not-so-voluntary and paid staff

Just as the charity retailing sector as a whole has undergone major changes since the mid-1980s, in many cases the staffing of charity shops has radically altered. However, as noted in Chapter 2, charity retailing is far from a homogenous sector, and changes in staffing reflect the complexities of the broadening continuum of different categories and management strategies in charity shops. This chapter examines the introduction of paid staff, as well as considering how best to make the most of a volunteer workforce and looking at new sources of volunteers for charity shops. Topics covered include the complexities of volunteers' motivations and needs, and their role in the charity shop's relationship with social and circulation of goods networks within the locality.

Understanding and making the most of volunteers

Given both the nature of volunteering and the transience of some charity shops, it is impossible to gain an accurate number of volunteers in charity shops, but various estimates show a clear growth in numbers in the 1990s, increasing from 50,000 (St Ledger 1993) to 100,000 (Mintel 1997) and 125,000 (Goodall 2000c). These some 125,000 volunteers contribute an estimated three quarters of a million work hours in charity shops in the UK each year (Goodall 2000c). Charity shop volunteers are part of a wider voluntary sector, but work in the niche of charity retailing, which is quite distinct from most other forms of fund-raising and voluntary work and is described by Goodall (2000c) as at the border between commercialism and retailing. Arguably, the same could be said for the League of Friends cafés and shops in hospitals throughout the UK and other countries, but what is distinct is the amount of turnover and consequent profits on trading. Charity shop volunteers alone contribute £150 million worth of work calculated at the minimum wage (Goodall 2000c), and in doing so are part of the wider financial equivalent contribution volunteers make to society. The Voluntary Centre UK estimated that the UK's 22 million volunteers contribute £41 billion to the GDP – more than the construction industry, for example (Ali 1996). Voluntary work, often intended to provide services in the community that are beyond the capacity of the government, relieves governments of the responsibility to provide millions of pounds worth of services, as well as contributing to strong and cohesive communities (Davis Smith 2000). 'By building trust and reciprocity between citizens, volunteering helps to create a more cohesive, stable society and a more economically prosperous one' (ibid.: 16). Given the potential combination of these factors accruing from the development of social capital within civil society, it is not surprising to find that the US and UK governments have been promoting voluntary work in a systematic way in the 1990s.

Voluntary work is generally defined as unpaid labour – or at least something not undertaken for financial gain, as there may be some payment, such as expenses – carried out for the benefit of someone outside one's own circles of kin (Davis Smith 2000; General Household Survey (GHS) 1992, Coding and Editing Notes, cited by Jarvis and Hancock 1997: 231). Most definitions exclude compulsion to 'volunteer' as being incompatible with the nature of voluntarism, but Davis Smith suggests there are exceptions that make this issue more complex, such as food-for-work schemes and obligatory community work by schoolchildren. The use of Community Service Order hours within charity shops (Maddrell 1999, 2000) and other arenas adds weight to the need to widen this definition of voluntarism, recognising some forms of volunteering to be a limited expression of agency within very significant structural (even legal) constraints.

About one-quarter of the UK adult population act as volunteers in some capacity, suggesting a total volunteer workforce of some 10.9 million adults (General Household Survey 1992 cited by Jarvis and Hancock 1997); but rates vary by age, gender, economic activity and ethnicity. Much voluntarism in industrialised countries in the past grew out of strong religious affiliation and conviction (especially where social responsibility was promoted), but nowadays it encompasses both a wide range of institutions and individuals with differing motivations (Sarfit and Merrill 2000; Lukka and Locke 2000). In their study of the USA and Canada, Sarfit and Merrill identify ten recent key trends in voluntarism, including increasing rates of volunteer burnout, increased competition between a growing number of charities for a falling number of volunteers and a trend to episodic rather than

continuous volunteering. These characteristics are also found to differing degrees within voluntarism in the UK and, more specifically,
most apply to the volunteer body within the charity shop sector.

Demographic studies of UK volunteers suggest that the most significant characteristics influencing volunteering are gender and age. Even
though women's employment patterns are becoming increasingly similar to men's, one in four women volunteer, compared to one in five
men. Those least likely to be volunteers are the very old, both men
and women (only one person in seven in the over 70 years age group;
Jarvis and Hancock (1997)). Jarvis and Hancock (1997) also noted that
more than a quarter of those surveyed preferred to give money rather
than time, a group that included one-third of unemployed men, reflecting the relatively low level of participation (18 per cent) in volunteering by the unemployed. This trend seems common to different ethnic
groups (see J. Foster's (1997) survey of volunteers from black and
ethnic minority communities in Britain, and Maddrell (2000)). More
work needs to be undertaken for us to understand the character of
ethnicity in voluntary work as a whole and in the charity shop sector.

While the increased number of women in paid work might suggest
that there could be a fall in the availability of volunteer hours, it was
found that it was those in employment who were most likely to do
voluntary work. The highest participation rate (46 per cent) in voluntary work was among those who were self-employed part time (Jarvis
and Hancock 1997). This potentially bodes well for voluntarism in
general as employment patterns move towards greater fragmentation,
but it may necessitate a clearer offering of episodic or workplace
volunteer opportunities in order to capture the limited time people
have or are prepared to offer in the face of alternative calls on their
time. This is especially the case for those already juggling career and
family responsibilities, but also applies to those of Generation X (born
1964–80), who tend to be protective of 'personal' time (Sarfit and
Merrill 2000). However, these trends are not necessarily helpful to
sustaining volunteer numbers in charity shops, as current opening
hours coincide with regular shop/work hours. It might be possible to
offer evening volunteer opportunities such as for collecting or sorting
donated goods, but this in turn would require longer management
hours (and hence increased costs).

Charity shop volunteer characteristics: who and why?

While charity shops are becoming increasingly professionalised (i.e.
using some paid staff and operating conventional formal retailing

Table 5.1 Number of volunteers and volunteer hours

Charity	Average number of volunteers per shop	Average hours worked per volunteer
Oxfam	26	5
British Heart Foundation	—	—
Imperial Cancer Research Fund	—	—
Help the Aged	12	4
SCOPE	10	8
Barnardo's	16	6
Cancer Research Campaign	19	5
British Red Cross	—	—
Sue Ryder	—	—
Age Concern	15	16
National Trust	—	—
Cards for Good Causes	22	—
Royal Society for the Protection of Birds	1.5	—
St Peter's Hospice Bristol	—	—
Trinity Hospice Shops	10	—
St Giles Hospice Shops	30	—

Source: After Phelan (1999)

practices), it generally remains true that in most of them the manager and assistant managers are the only paid members of staff, resulting in much of the work of the UK's some 6,000 charity shops being undertaken by a volunteer workforce.

Volunteers have been described as charities' 'lifeblood', and the charity shop's greatest asset (Horne and Broadbridge 1995), largely because they perform two main functions: fund-raising and providing a link between the charity and the general public (St Leger 1993). The value of volunteer labour in charity shops has been estimated as worth twice the sector's profits (Goodall 2000c), hence a very significant economic contribution, but volunteer labour is both less and more than the apparent financial asset (Maddrell 2000). Attempts have begun to assign some accounting value to the work of volunteers, which has numerous parallels with recent attempts by the UK government to give economic value to unpaid domestic labour (ibid.), the most effective of which is Volunteer Investment and Value Audit (VIVA).[1] VIVA is based on assigning a market value to volunteers' work (at local gendered pay rates for equivalent types of activity), assessing volunteer management costs and calculating the ratio between these

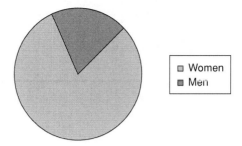

Figure 5.1 Percentage of charity shop volunteers by gender (Oxford)
Source: Maddrell (2000)

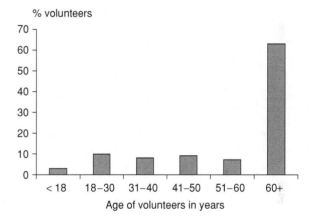

Figure 5.2 Percentage of volunteers by age category (Oxford)
Source: Maddrell (2000)

two to provide the VIVA cost-effectiveness ratio – that is, the economic
return on each pound invested in volunteers in terms of training and
management (Gaskin 1997). However, although the most effective
measure, the VIVA method can be accurately applied only at local or
regional level, meaning that it could be evaluated by managers in
individual charity shops or within particular charity chains, but that it
is very difficult to quantify in generalist terms across such a diverse
sector (Maddrell 2000). If we take economic significance alone as an
indicator of the value of volunteer work to national and community
life (and international life in the case of charity shops raising money
for overseas), it is possible to place an approximate but quantifiable
value on volunteers. Their value as community links for retailing and

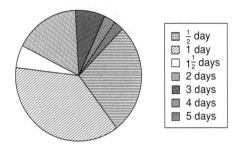

Figure 5.3 Days volunteered by percentage of volunteers (Oxford)
Source: Maddrell (2000)

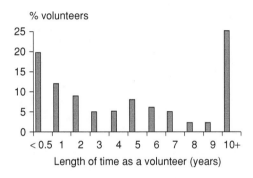

Figure 5.4 Volunteers' length of service (Oxford)
Source: Maddrell (2000)

other local fund-raising as well as broader charity service is less tangible but can be of equal value to the mission of the charity.

Those inclined to volunteer but not committed to a particular charitable cause are frequently influenced to approach a local charity shop simply by dint of its proximity. In contrast to most managers, the majority of volunteers live within two miles of the shop where they volunteer, for example 60 per cent of volunteers surveyed by Horne and Broadbridge (1994) and 54 per cent of volunteer respondents compared to only 2 of the 17 managers in Oxford (Maddrell 2000). It is by dint of their localness that volunteers bring 'added value' to the charity shop beyond their replacement cost. Volunteers act as the primary link between other people in the locality and the charity, and therefore, through these social relations, mediate between the charity and community, embedding both the *functional* and the *symbolic* space of the charity shop within the locality. This is largely done by the creation of an expressive order within the locale of the shop (see Dickens 1990), when (if) the collective sociation of those working in the shop extends to encompass donors, customers and neighbouring visitors. Volunteers are central to achieving this and thus constitute an important component in the whole charity retail circulation process (Maddrell 2000).

The earliest major study of charity shop volunteers (looking at a single large charity chain of shops in Scotland) showed that the majority of volunteer respondents surveyed were female, white, over the age of 55, either married or widowed, retired, and without formal educational qualifications (Horne and Broadbridge 1994). This image of the charity shop volunteer falls within the traditional stereotype of volunteer as the middle-class older selfless woman with time available to do good works for the poor (the Victorian 'angel in the house' (Poovey 1988)) (Maddrell 2000).

The 'angel in the house' image is borne out by the fact that charity shop volunteers are overwhelmingly female: 80 per cent of volunteer respondents in Oxford (see Figure 5.1) (Maddrell 2000), 92 per cent in the Isle of Man (Maddrell 2001b), 95 per cent in Ruislip (Whithear 1999), 98 per cent in the Scottish chain studied by Horne and Broadbridge (1994), with many charity shop managers identifying only one or two men in the corps of volunteers. This is very different from the general pattern of volunteering, in which rates of male volunteering are at most 20 per cent lower than those of women, and raises the question as to why this gendered pattern of volunteering occurs in charity shops.

Some men do act as general shop volunteers; others commonly offer a particular professional service for which they are qualified. Examples range between accountancy, expertise in valuing and/or mending high-value products such as cameras, antiques, records and other collectables, electrical and other shop-fitting work, and van driving for door-to-door collection of bagged donations. These are jobs that are often done on an irregular or *ad hoc* basis (Maddrell 2000) – different forms of episodic volunteering. It has been suggested that the sale and purchasing of second-hand clothes is largely a female activity (Gregson and Crewe 1998), which may account for gendered patterns of volunteering in charity shops; certainly charity shops have been perceived as a feminine space by both volunteers and shoppers. However, the fact that many charity shops have professionalised and moved away from the musty second-hand clothes image may account, in part, for the significant recent increase of male volunteers (Maddrell

2000), as has the small but growing number of male managers, who report success in recruiting young men as shop volunteers. Hegemonic masculine arenas found at car boot sales, such as gardening, DIY and car spares and accessories (Gregson and Crewe 1998), are not to be found in charity shops, but alternatives can be found in the form of specialist outlets such as bookshops, which attract a high proportion of male volunteers (Maddrell 2000). American thrift shops similarly tend to be female dominated, but a growing number of not-for-profit thrift shops raising funds for Aids charities are noted for the large number of male volunteers (often gay men), such as Phili-thrift for Aids in Philadelphia (Maddrell 2000). As yet there are no permanent Aids-related charity shops in the UK, although there have been temporary shops selling Elton John's surplus clothes in 1996 and 2001 to raise money for the Terrence Higgins Trust.[2] The trend towards the professionalisation of the volunteer workforce, in terms of the use of volunteers with professional skills, combined with changing work and retirement patterns (identified by Sarfit and Merrill (2000)) and use of community service hours (see below), are serving to masculinise the volunteer workforce and potentially the space of the charity shop, especially where specialist shops are attracting both male vounteers and male consumers.

Members of the public make themselves available for voluntary work in charity shops for a number of reasons. Some are motivated by concern for, or experience of, the charity's particular focus; this is especially the case of medical charities. Volunteers are also motivated by more general reasons, both altruistic and personal. Voluntarism has been characterised as incorporating four main (overlapping) categories based on outcome: mutual aid, service to others, participation in governance, and advocacy (Davis Smith 2000). Charity shop volunteers are occupied in the service of others – that is, philanthropy, albeit indirect. However, while they may not be the main beneficiaries, they do often accrue benefits: 'most people would acknowledge that there is some element of self-interest in all philanthropic activity' (ibid.: 12). A national survey of voluntary activity in the UK showed that the majority of volunteers became involved for reasons associated with their own needs in some way (Lynn and Davis Smith 1991). One charity shop volunteer attested, 'I lost both of my parents to cancer, so it is close to my heart' (Volunteer 16, Oxford Q). McClelland's (1961) motivation typology of need fulfilment, although limited, seems to relate to many charity shop volunteers who indicate the need for affiliation and need for achievement as significant motivators. The third type of need, need for power, is less obvious – although it may underlie some conflicts between volunteers and paid managers when the latter exert their authority over previously 'equal' volunteers. Other need types, such as play, nurturance, construction, deference, safety, love, esteem, self-actualisation and self-transcendence (see Oliver 1997: 140–2), can also be identified in volunteers' responses and practice.

While charity shop volunteers are predominantly motivated by a desire to support the charitable cause, especially in the case of medical charities (Maddrell 2000), the increasingly diverse body of volunteers has equally varied motives – both altruistic and personal. Fifty-seven per cent of volunteer respondents in the Isle of Man were motivated by the particular charitable cause, but such motivation was less significant in both Ruislip and Oxford (30 per cent and 28 per cent respectively). At 28 per cent, the desire to support the *particular* charity was the leading motivation for volunteers in Oxford, but only 4 per cent of volunteers cited an *actual personal* association with the charity where they were working, and these respondents were all working for either a medical or a hospice charity shop (ibid.). In the face of increased competition for volunteers within the sector, volunteer loyalty to the cause or the locale of the shop has become a significant issue for managers. Individual charities such as hospice charities, the Save the Children Fund, cancer charities and Oxfam each achieved a high degree of loyalty on the part of volunteers, in part reflecting the strength of the charity's mission and volunteers' identification with this. Such 'loyalty to the cause' can also relate to loyalty to place: while some volunteers were motivated specifically to 'help the Third World', others wanted to support local charities, notably hospices (ibid.). In cases of local causes, there is a much greater sense of mutual aid, the idea that this fund-raising through charity shops benefits the immediate community if not necessarily the individual volunteer (at present). While not unique to the Isle of Man, this loyalty to place took on a particular character there (by definition, an island is a bounded place). Some volunteer (and many customer) respondents there stressed the importance of supporting a local charity and being a part of local networks and social relations: 'Retired early. Manx charity money stays on [the] island. Enjoy meeting regular customers' (Volunteer 4, Isle of Man L). However, the sense of supporting local and 'home' national charities was a recurring theme for both volunteers and charity shoppers, especially where there was a strong sense of local or regional identity.

The overwhelming majority of volunteer respondents in Ruislip (63 per cent) chose to work in a charity shop 'to do something useful' and 'meet other people' (Whithear 1999). This general altruism influenced 18 per cent of the Oxford sample and was matched by the desire for company (18 per cent) on the part of volunteers (Maddrell 2000). Eighty per cent of those citing the need for company as a key reason for volunteering were over 60 years of age (the dominant age group). Similarly, in the Oxford study virtually all of those respondents who volunteered to occupy spare time, 'keep active' (either mentally or physically), or as an antidote to boredom or loneliness were aged over 60 years. However, reasons of this kind are not always age related as females aged under 45 and in paid employment were primarily motivated to volunteer in order to meet people and make friends (Horne and Broadbridge 1994). These social needs may also relate to the fact that fewer than half of volunteers surveyed in Oxford, for example, have a current/living partner (Maddrell 2000).

Enjoying shop work and/or the particular products sold influenced a significant minority of volunteers (8 per cent in Oxford), particularly in specialist charity outlets such as bookshops.

> 'The opportunity presented itself when my husband who worked for [the charity] told me about it and I had enjoyed shop work so much that I knew not only would I enjoy it, but the money raised would be used for helping others and making life happier for them.'
> (Volunteer 12, Oxford R)

It is increasingly common to find volunteers having previous experience in retailing: estimates range between 20 per cent (Broadbridge and Horne 1996), 37 per cent (Whithear 1999) and 41 per cent (Maddrell 2000) of volunteer respondents. This trend perhaps reflects the preference of paid (usually retail-trained) managers for volunteers already versed in the skills and ethos of retailing. Similarly, those with retail experience (and often lacking other formal qualifications) may feel particularly empowered to contribute to charity retailing as opposed to other forms of voluntary work (Maddrell 2000). As such, these retail-experienced volunteers (mostly women) should be seen as 'professional' volunteers alongside the accountants and the like who are generally recognised as bringing a professional skill to their volunteering.

While the Canadian government promotes voluntary work as a means of skills development and career exploration for young adults (Sarfit and Merrill 2000), and studies have shown a link between voluntary work and employability (Davis Smith 2000), in the UK a relatively small number of volunteers are influenced by the desire to gain work experience. For example, only 6 per cent of Oxford volunteers sought work experience, perhaps reflecting the age profile of volunteers (see below), although a further 5 per cent used volunteering as a means of gaining confidence in their personal lives (Maddrell 2000).

> 'I have had problems with my health for the past 13 years, and I suffered a number of major breakdowns in my early 20s. It is something to do, which is for a good cause and has given me good experience. I hope to get a part-time paid job in a gift shop soon.'
>
> (Volunteer 5, Oxford J)

However, in areas of higher unemployment, such as Liverpool, there is more evidence of the use of charity shop volunteering as a stepping stone to employment.

Voluntary work is increasingly recognised as a means of aiding therapy and/or recovery from illness,[3] and is often clearly linked to life cycle stages. A variety of therapeutic reasons occur, including mental and physical illness, drug rehabilitation, bereavement, or as a means of recovering the volunteer's own sense of identity and empowerment (Maddrell 2000): 'because I want to give time and can't give money' (Volunteer 8, Oxford J); 'spare time which I like to use helping. My grandparents had cancer and I'd like to make up for not being able to help them' (Volunteer 1, Isle of Man J).

However, some volunteers can be influenced by very idiosyncratic personal preferences, exemplified by one volunteer who decided where to offer her services in part according to the image of the shop (something more usually associated with influencing customers' purchasing patterns): 'Out of all the charity shops I decided on this one, as it helps the elderly and the window is always nicely dressed – not cluttered up' (Volunteer 2, Isle of Man O).

Largely based around a minimum of a weekly four-hour shift (Broadbridge and Horne 1996; Phelan 1999b; Maddrell 2000), charity shop volunteering clearly qualifies as an 'intensive' form of volunteering, 'intensive' volunteers being defined as those people who have done voluntary work on at least twenty days in the previous year (Lynn and Davis Smith 1991). However, there appears to be a trend towards a significant minority of charity shop volunteers working for more than 12 hours per week (Maddrell 2000). While having a high number of volunteer labour hours provided by a small number of people tends to lead to volunteer 'burn-out' (Sarfit and Merrill 2000), this does depend upon the 'type' of volunteer, their motives and the work undertaken. Although defined as 'intensive' when defined by time commitment, charity shop work does not have the physical or emotional demands of some other forms of voluntary work, such as providing support services for the terminally ill, so is less emotionally intensive. Furthermore, volunteers seeking social interaction, or licensed prisoners on day release from prison, welcome and benefit from the opportunity to be working in the charity shop environment for longer periods of time.

Time given to volunteering is one area where male volunteer respondents appear to differ from the overall sample. Combined figures for male volunteers in charity shops in Oxford and the Isle of Man show that 40 per cent gave a *maximum* of one half-day per week, compared to 26 per cent of the overall sample (this was not affected by men's participation in paid work, which was parallel to the overall sample, with 7 per cent undertaking part-time work). Ten per cent of male respondents volunteered for a full five days per week, but these men were all licensed prisoners completing community service work on day release in Oxford (see below). The latter were also all under 40 years of age, thereby skewing the age profile of male volunteers, with 27 per cent of male volunteers in general being under 40 years and 53 per cent over 60 years of age (subtracting prisoner 'volunteers' from the sample showed the age distribution of male volunteers to reflect the general pattern) (Maddrell 2000).

Many of the longest-serving volunteers are over retirement age and have worked at their particular shop since it opened, suggesting the importance of initial recruitment when a new shop opens (Maddrell 2000) (see Figure 5.4). Longevity of service by a volunteer corps has been associated with charity shops that are volunteer managed (Whithear 1999), suggesting high levels of sociation and loyalty to cause and/or manager in these instances. This clearly has implications for management of shops, notably raising issues about sustainable patterns of volunteer recruitment, with retention and replacement of volunteers in the medium term needing attention, even allowing for short-term volunteers such as students and New Deal placements. While evidence suggests that charity shops have a fairly stable core of volunteers, most shops are always in need of volunteers and the cost of turnover is high (Broadbridge and Horne 1996; Mintel 1997).

Managers describe the ideal volunteer complement to be four for each morning and afternoon shift (two for the front shop and two for the back room). On the basis of half-day shifts, this would require a pool of forty-eight volunteers for each week. In reality, few shops have the desired number of volunteers – only one shop in the Oxford survey, with several shops in the sample running on a complement of six to twelve volunteers, in contrast to earlier suggestions of an average of thirty-five volunteers per shop (Broadbridge and Horne 1996). In 1998 the Imperial Cancer Research Fund ran the SOS (Staff Our Shop) campaign, which included leaflets and complete window displays devoted to the volunteer recruitment drive; other charities such as Help the Aged and SCOPE have included a plea for volunteers on every price label.

In keeping with the broader volunteer sector, charity shop volunteers tend to be recruited via informal interaction linkages (for example, through the lobbying of friends and word of mouth) as opposed to source linkages such as advertisements, with 60 per cent of volunteers first hearing of the opportunity through informal channels, representing a significantly higher proportion than those recruited to formal retailing (Broadbridge and Horne 1996). Managers report more reliance on word of mouth for volunteer recruitment, suggesting that informal links develop as the shop becomes established (ibid.), particularly as the shop becomes embedded in the social relations of local communities. Whithear (1999) reported the significance of person-to-person 'concentric circle recruitment', particularly in volunteer-managed shops that rely on informal networks. This was seen to be particularly evident in charity shops in the Isle of Man (Maddrell 2001b). However, its significance varies between and within areas: while Oxford volunteer responses suggested a low level of this form of recruitment, the Salvation Army shop, with its close links to the church, had a high degree of volunteer linkage. Often volunteers experience 'an important and lengthy process between hearing about a volunteer opportunity and actualising it. Many people slip into volunteering' (Broadbridge and Horne 1996: 321). This is also reflected in the often varied motives reported by individual volunteers and the group as a whole, some being prompted initially by a friend or an appeal, but then joining somewhere and at some time that suits their own convenience and motivations. A significant feature of this emerging volunteer culture is the extent to which volunteers sometimes need to gain as much from their voluntary work as they in turn provide themselves (as seen in their varied motivations). This can be expensive to the charity in terms of training and/or supervision, but has become necessary in the face of competition between charity shops. However, where there is sufficient return to the charities in terms of hours worked or longevity of service, this can be to the mutual reward of both volunteers and the charity shop (Maddrell 2000).

Where charity shops are grounded in the local community – what might be described as 'organic', grown out of local interest – shop managers are able to draw on a reserve of volunteers through local contacts (Maddrell 2000). Small operators, especially local hospice shops, appear less susceptible than large chains to the difficulties of attracting volunteers (as well as donated goods) because of strong local loyalties (Phelan 1997) – a relationship clearly demonstrated in Parsons's (1996) study of different types of charity shops in Bristol. Reliance on informal means of recruitment tends to increase the homogeneity of the volunteer pool (Broadbridge and Horne 1996), particularly when drawing on local friendship networks: 'In a place like this, if you're short, you just ask your friends in the WI [Women's Institute] and they come and help' (Manager I, Isle of Man).

While personal invitation may be the most effective means of recruitment, it tends to perpetuate volunteer characteristics in terms of race, gender and class (Sarfit and Merrill 2000). This may not be appropriate in an increasingly ethnically and culturally diverse society (Sarfit and Merrill 2000). Indeed, it may be alienating to potential volunteers as well as customers, but volunteer recruiters should be wary of over-burdening those already struggling to make ends meet (Davis Smith 2000).

While individual shops have their own particular character and therefore their own attractions and strategies for recruiting volunteers, in part reflecting the type of charity, all charity shop managers have responsibility for recruitment of volunteers as part of their job description. For example, some charity chains, such as PDSA (the People's Dispensary for Sick Animals), formally contract managers to spend one day each month on recruiting volunteers through local contacts and charity-related interest groups. Recruitment is a major task, as attracting reliable volunteers can be difficult, especially in areas of near-full employment. For example, the original Oxfam shop on Broad Street in Oxford city centre was reported to be threatened with closure due to a lack of volunteers (*The Times*, 3 March 1997) (Maddrell 2000).

The volunteer contribution

The relationship between any charity shop and the people of its surrounding locality or community is reciprocal, not least as the shop relies on keeping the locals 'sweet', both for sales and as an element in the shop's supply chain of donated goods. This might be achieved through careful marketing to the locality if the impetus for the shop was not local in the first instance, or it can be developed as a form of social relations, whereby the charity shop and its functions become an *integrated* part of the, or create their own, local social system (see Chapter 7).

Volunteers are important not only for processing, (re)presenting and selling goods in the shop, but also as a supply of goods, both personally – 'they are always fetching bits and pieces' (Manager P, Oxford) – and through functioning as conduits for local donations. Volunteers have a very high participation rate in both donating and buying goods from the shops where they volunteer; for example, 91 per cent of Oxford volunteers donated to and 95 per cent purchased goods from the shop where they volunteered – although this does not give any idea of the actual *quantity* of goods. Interestingly, while male volunteers[4] were as likely as the general sample group to donate goods, they were 10–15 per cent less likely to be consumers of charity shop goods – although one male respondent cited access to cheap goods as a key motive for personally volunteering: '(i) to obtain cheap secondhand clothing, shirts, shoes, etc. (ii) voluntary work can be put down on my CV' (Volunteer 13, Oxford R).

The 1980s have been characterised in the retailing sector (as elsewhere) by profit maximisation and designer interiors; however, the 'caring 90s' saw a return to 'customer care' in some retail sectors (facilitated by time-saving electronic processing and stock control). This is especially true of upmarket niche retailers who are up-skilling their sales assistants, compared to the simultaneous down-skilling and minimal decor of downmarket outlets (Crewe and Lowe 1996). Charity shop volunteers, along with managers, have been observed offering levels of customer care not usually experienced outside the expensive niche market shops, and rarely found in cut-price shops, which constitute the main competitors for charity shops. Giving this attention to individuals is commonly part of the charity shop ethos, and in so doing volunteers can act as an important element in attracting and retaining customers (Maddrell 2000). One charity shop volunteer described the attraction of the shop where he worked: 'A very popular venue for many regular customers who appreciate value for *money and pleasant service*; many visitors appreciate these also' (Volunteer 3, Isle of Man P) (respondent's emphasis).

The charity shop can play an important community role in providing somewhere for people to meet or take part in social interaction, especially the lonely, but this function is largely dependent upon the attitude of the manager and goodwill of volunteers (Maddrell 2000; see also Chapter 3). '[The charity shop is] a meeting place for the lonely – we as volunteers can chat, give them a few minutes of our time' (Volunteer 2 , Isle of Man D). This is in keeping with the policy in Sue Ryder shops, for example, which states that every customer should be made to feel welcome, cherished and important (Sue Ryder 1992), and Age Concern's mission to meet the needs of the elderly. Arguably this approach can also be seen as a clever sales strategy, and one recently rediscovered by consumer-oriented shops such as The Gap and the Body Shop (see Crewe and Lowe 1996). The approach can be seen as accommodating people in such a way that they feel comfortable in the shop and will return to browse and shop at leisure. It is this offering over and above the obvious merchandise that makes the charity shop a special and different retail institution (Horne and Broadbridge 1995: c.2.3) – and volunteers are vital to this, especially volunteers with local knowledge and social networks.

The preponderance of female volunteers and the nature of their contribution to charity shop functions may appear to support the image of the volunteer as the 'angel in the shop', but the variety of motives on the part of volunteers suggests a more complex and heterogeneous group (if not necessarily a socially diverse one). Matching the needs of these volunteers with those of the charity shops, and the ensuing management implications, are addressed below. Wider issues in using volunteers as the main source of labour hours in charity shops include the limitations of what volunteers are prepared to do (hours, tasks, follow directives, training, etc.) and the shortage of volunteers/volunteer hours in the face of growing competition within the voluntary sector as a whole and charity shops in particular (see Figure 5.3) (Maddrell 2000). 'There are not enough volunteers, they are too thinly spread and there is competition from other charity shops' (Area Manager Q, Oxfordshire).

There is also the issue of balancing the social needs of the volunteers (as well as some customers) against the overall task of raising funds for the charity. Volunteers are seen by charities as giving 'legitimacy' to the process of converting donations to profit, but the pressure of turnover targets does not always sit easily with managing a volunteer workforce (Whithear 1999). It has also been suggested that pressure to meet sales targets set by area managers has reduced some volunteers' pleasure in their work, causing some to defect to less pressured neighbouring competitors, although others have been proud of their contribution to the attaining of targets (Manager P, Oxford). How these questions are approached often depends upon the combined factors of charity and manager ethos in charity retailing: whether volunteers are seen as being there solely for the charity, or the charity is seen as being there, in part, for the volunteers (strident commercialism or professional voluntarism; Goodall (2000c)). This in turn can be seen in terms of whether volunteers are valued or not and whether they are largely structured or have a high degree of participative agency.

By its very nature, volunteer work is dependent upon the goodwill of the volunteers. This has made it difficult to impose certain new work practices within the voluntary sector, and charities are responding by introducing more formal interviewing processes, accompanied by job descriptions and even formal contracts in some cases (Maddrell 2000). Training has been seen as both a solution and problem in itself for charity management, and is at the heart of the question and practice of applying formal retail procedures to charity retailing – what many identify as the professionalisation of charity retailing. Volunteers often do not wish to be seen as staff, can be unwilling to conform to bureaucratic procedures (Ilsley 1990) and resist formal training. This clashes with the increased regularisation of voluntary agencies in the UK in recent years, particularly as a result of European Union legal, health and safety regulations. Volunteers, especially long-termers who often resent the idea of training *per se*, are especially resistant to paperwork tasks, which they see as detracting from the 'real job' and/ or requiring extra input (ibid.). 'We've been doing it our way – why mend it when it's not broken? . . . [the extra paperwork] comes from a little man in the attic with nothing better to do' (Volunteer 12, Liverpool H).

Typically, two-thirds of volunteers receive some degree of training (Broadbridge and Horne 1996; Maddrell 2000), but rates vary between shops, as do perceptions of what constitutes training, as in the case of the 3 per cent of the volunteers in the Oxford survey who said they had not been given training in the shop but went on to describe themselves as receiving training 'on the job' (Maddrell 2000). Training in charity shops relates primarily to immediate business needs (Broadbridge and Horne 1996; Whithear 1999; Maddrell 2000) (see Figure 5.5), with female and male volunteers receiving training in much the same areas (Maddrell 2000), although it appears that charity shop volunteers receive a narrower range of training than other retail distribution staff (Broadbridge and Horne 1996). However, this picture needs to be placed in the context of the preferences of many volunteers to undertake a limited range of activities with which they feel comfortable (some prefer back-room work, for example). There are also difficulties in making time to train numerous staff who work only for relatively few hours, especially when there is resistance to the principle of training. The involvement of increased numbers of volunteers with previous retail experience also renders some training unnecessary. However, it should also be noted that the offer of training

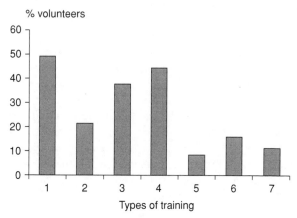

Figure 5.5 Types of training received by Oxford charity shop volunteers. Key: 1 Till; 2 steaming; 3 sorting; 4 pricing; 5 book-keeping; 6 display; 7 other

Source: Maddrell (2000)

could be a positive incentive for those seeking skills and/or career development (especially young people, or those embarking on a return to work, or unemployed people) and this is an area to exploit in recruitment of these groups.

The move to increasingly professionalised retail practices in charity shops – for example, stock control and rotation; security tagging in some cases; Electronic Point of Sale (EPOS) equipment, sometimes necessary when new goods are sold; higher-profile uniform branding; and the increasing availability of credit card payment – can present new training challenges. However, this is commonly addressed by means of a division of labour within the workforce, often leaving the majority of volunteers to undertake the unskilled aspects of running the shop (Maddrell 2000). Managers have reported tensions with volunteers over a range of issues relating broadly to professionalised practices intended to improve the image of the shop and increase sales (ibid.). Volunteers have frequently objected to charities spending money on improved shop decor and display, although this discomfort was usually alleviated when improved sales figures were subsequently attained. Similarly, directives from charity headquarters banning eating, chatting and even sitting at the till were deeply resented, but where rules were considered inappropriate they were subverted or ignored by volunteers: 'They're not stopping me from sitting down' (Volunteer 11, Oxford J) (ibid.).

Widening the volunteer pool

Demand for volunteers to work in charity shops has matched the growth of the sector as a whole, resulting in competition for volunteers, especially where shops are clustered. Hence charity shop managers have been seeking new methods of recruitment to create a more diverse base of volunteers (Broadbridge and Horne 1996). Some charity shops have initiated innovative solutions to meet this demand. The problem has been addressed by different charities and individual shop managers in differing ways, including advertising the fact that expenses are paid and training given, being responsive to volunteer needs and motivations, as well as tapping new sources of volunteers (Maddrell 2000).

Recognising the social needs of volunteers and consciously acknowledging their contribution to the charity can be seen in those charities where recognition is given through annual magazine reports and prizes (Sue Ryder, for example) or recognition of length of service, such as annual badges in Help the Aged and five-year commendation badges and certificates of service in SCOPE, paralleling the practice within other voluntary and commercial agencies, such as badges given by blood donor banks and some supermarket retailers.

Linking rewards to motivations for volunteering can be seen in the case of charity chains that offer 'perks' to volunteers. Some shops give volunteers discount on goods (although it has been suggested that they do so in part to reduce pilfering). Help the Aged emphasises social activities for volunteers, including organised outings and holidays, but it is more common for charity shops to organise an annual event such as Christmas dinner, which often doubles as a thank-you to volunteers from the charity itself. Social activities are particularly significant given the low participation rate of volunteers in community activities in some areas: only 39 per cent of Oxford respondents participated in organisations offering formal social activities within the community such as churches, the Women's Institute, political constituency parties and sports groups, although the figure was much higher at 59 per cent in the Isle of Man. This would appear to support the trend identified in the USA of declining civic participation in general, but increased volunteering since the 1970s (see Goss 1999). As noted above, many volunteers see their work in the charity shop as an intrinsically social activity: '[I volunteered] to obviate loneliness and boredom (which it does, I find it fun!)' (Volunteer 2, Isle of Man M).

When volunteers are experiencing their voluntary work as a means of identity formation, identifying with the cause and their fellow workers, there are grounds for a strong sense of sociation. This is particularly true when this is overlain by additional social activities with fellow volunteers, in which case there is a blurring of the boundaries between voluntary labour and leisure/pleasure (reflecting the often mixed motives of volunteers in undertaking their voluntary work in the first instance – as indicated above). The role of the charity shop as a centre of mutual support can be seen particularly in the case of pensioner, mental health and other medical charities. As one manager pointed out, 'All my volunteers have had some contact with cancer – some of the women *have* breast cancer, but they are not always the best volunteers as they are not always fit for a full shift of work' (Manager Q, Oxford). However, managers, no matter how willing, are scarcely finding the time for supporting staff, let alone customers with charity-related needs (Maddrell 2000). The same manager explained the tensions between the priority of fund-raising and giving support to volunteers and customers, suggesting that professionalism (in terms of fund-raising) was becoming the primary concern, rather than delivering charitable support through the space of the shop: 'pressures from HQ to meet targets etc. means there is less time for that sort of service to the community' (Manager Q, Oxford).

The reimbursement of expenses and provision of training should accommodate potential volunteers for whom volunteering may be financially or personally expensive, thereby becoming more socially inclusive. However, within much of the sector there is a general culture of volunteers not claiming expenses (Maddrell 2000). While failure to claim expenses may be seen as part of an individual's voluntary contribution to the charity if he or she can afford it, it is divisive in marking out as different those who do need to claim expenses. In practice this appears not to be an issue for those 'compelled' to undertake their voluntary work, for example through those claiming Job Seeker's Allowance or undertaking a Community Service Order, but going against the cultural practices of the shop could be socially embarrassing for other types of volunteers, unless it is sensitively mediated by the manager.

Another approach to remedying volunteer shortage is through widening the volunteer pool as a form of mutual 'community service' between the charity shop and particular groups in the community (Maddrell 2000). Such groups include school, further and higher education students who have some element of 'community service' within their curriculum or extra-curricular activities – for example, those trying to achieve the Duke of Edinburgh Award – as well as those looking for work placements for qualifications in retailing or voluntary sector management.

Charity shop managers also use volunteers referred by social workers (often through agencies such as the Council for Voluntary Service). 'One client lives by her Wednesday afternoon ironing. She gets first look at the bargains. They have basically invented a job to keep her busy' (Social Worker S, Liverpool). Volunteers referred by social services or from the charity's own sponsoring body may have difficulty finding paid employment because of physical disability, mental health problems, drug rehabilitation or low self-esteem, but can be found therapeutic occupation within the charity shop, often through single-skill activities (Maddrell 2000). The challenges and rewards of working with these volunteers are exemplified by the following extracts from manager interviews:

'We've got two volunteers through social services . . . it's to help get them into the community. One has no reading or writing, she does practical jobs, bin cleaning, silver, etc. The other can read and goes on the till. They probably volunteer for about a day a week.'
(Manager R, Oxford)

'We have two volunteers from [the sponsoring charity], one has really come on over the years, come out of herself . . . the other pins on one label and has to sit down. She needs a lot of supervision, but we keep her in view of us.'
(Assistant Manager I, Oxford)

Another innovative category of 'volunteer' is the least voluntary. These are people who have been convicted of an offence and sentenced to a Community Service Order (CSO) under the supervision of the probation service or are licensed prisoners who are granted day release from open prison prior to parole in order to undertake unpaid community service work (Maddrell 2000). These groups have come to represent a significant number of staffing hours in some charity shops and therefore represent both an important managerial issue and an interesting aspect of social relations between charity shops and their locality.[5]

The UK Home Office does not have official figures to indicate the number of probation services or prisons using charity shop placements but informal surveys have shown the use of community service hours in charity shops to be a nation-wide, if far from uniform, phenomenon. There is similar use of probation hours in not-for-profit thrift shops in the USA. The use of community service hours seems to be a particularly well-developed mechanism within the Oxford area, and the following analysis focuses on research undertaken with probation officers, community service workers, prison officers and licensed prisoners working in charity shops in Oxford, as well as the managers and volunteers in those shops.

According to UK national standards, community service workers (CSWs), by law, should undertake demanding unpaid work for the community in a positive way as a form of reparation, but at the same time 'should not displace labour and should only undertake work that could not be done in any other way' (Keele Conference, cited by Whitfield and Scott 1993). The particular requirements for community service make charity shops an obvious placement, especially for mature first-time offenders (Probation Officer X, Oxford Probation Service (OPS)). Those sentenced to CSOs are usually given the option of two or more activities, and in Oxford, in 1997–8, some one-third of those probationers placed on individual community service placements (as opposed to group projects) were in charity shops. Similarly, in February 1998, 22 of 40 licensed prisoners (LPs) on pre-parole day release community service from Springhill Open Prison were working in charity shops (or warehouses) in the Oxfordshire area. In the case of both probationers and licensed prisoners, the 'volunteers' are carefully screened for suitability by their probation officer or pre-parole board and placed in response to charity shop requests and at a distance from anyone who may have been a victim of their previous offences.

Starting with one charity shop and spreading to others (e.g. by manager transfer), CSWs have been placed in charity shops in Oxford since the early 1990s, and by 1998 the majority of charity shops in Oxford had had a CSW or LP working for them. However, none publicises the fact (indeed, some shop managers do not inform their area manager!), largely owing to fear of damage to the brand image of the charity through adverse media coverage and/or public opinion.

CSW respondents were 77 per cent male, and 73 per cent were aged under 30 years (in contrast to 19 per cent and 11 per cent respectively of the charity shop volunteer sample). The majority of offences related to driving, 46 per cent being convicted of drunk driving and other driving offences, but the range of offences included fraud, theft, shoplifting, possession of drugs, being under the influence of excess alcohol, assault, criminal damage and handling stolen goods. By comparison, the licensed prisoners were all male (from a male prison), with eight of the ten being over 30 years of age; five were convicted of drugs offences, the others including burglary, theft and fraud, with sentences ranging between two and nine years (all had served time in 'closed' category B prisons prior to being placed in the open prison). The combined effect of the presence of CSWs and LPs makes for a much younger male element in the charity shop workforce. The costs and benefits of using these CSWs and LPs, as illustrated by the Oxford study, are evaluated below.

Commonly, people with convictions for driving offences, or probationer CSW 'volunteers', often prefer the more arduous but more anonymous back-room work (sorting, steaming, bagging) rather than being in the front of the shop, reinforcing the distinction between back- and front-room work (see Chapter 1). 'There are some very nice people – they make a nice atmosphere in the sordid back room' (Manager Q, Oxford). By comparison, LPs often prefer more varied work and often, once established, welcome opportunities to meet and work with people, whether as part of the volunteer team or in front-of-shop activities, as one interviewee summarised: '[I have most enjoyed] dealing with the public – I've never done that before, it's been a new experience for me' (LP 1, Oxford).

There is clearly the potential for discomfort and unease between other volunteers and those undertaking community service work. However, on the whole, other volunteers seem generally to respond well to CSWs and LPs, often seeing support of these 'volunteers' as part of their own service to the community – part of their discourse of charity in a wider sense:

'We have people on probation (community service) and young people from [a drug rehabilitation centre] community; we give them the chance to work in a team so they gain confidence.'

(Volunteer 4, Oxford J)

'They help increase the figures [the takings]. I make them part of the team. It's a whole new aspect of life for them [prisoners], they are quite extraordinary. . . . All volunteers want the figures up; our turnover has nearly doubled in two years, so the volunteers accept the community service people – we need them, especially in the back room. Some volunteers think it's Christian to look after, sympathise with, help the prisoners – an extension of their charity.'

(Manager Q, Oxford)

Perhaps surprisingly, the presence of reliable LPs – all men – is also welcomed by volunteers as added security in what can be an elderly feminised environment (Maddrell 2000):

'It's wonderful for us to have them around security-wise. We have a problem with Irish tinkers, but there's no problem if they're around – they see them on the till. Probably because of their background they're also aware of anyone dodgy. They call on the intercom for back-up or [for someone else to be] watching.'

(Manager J, Oxford)

While benefits range from professional skills, physical strength and even 'masculine presence', ultimately the key contribution of those doing community service hours to charity shops can be identified in increased takings as a result of their input, something recognised by managers, volunteers and CSWs or LPs alike.

CSWs in turn may benefit from their placements, through gaining work experience, including the discipline of work hours, with the potential for attendant motivation and increased self-esteem. Some benefit from in-shop perks. But the key gain, for LPs in particular, is often the experience of being accepted and working as part of a team in a 'normal' situation. '[They get on] because people don't talk about prison and it helps them get back into the community' (Manager M, Oxford). For some probationer CSWs, the main advantage of a place-ment in a charity shop was *not* being on probation group project work; as an individual placement, the charity shop allows distance, including avoiding mixing with 'seriously dodgy characters'.

However, just as the training and supervision of all staff, whether paid or unpaid, has a cost, there are costs (largely managerial) and limitations involved with the use of CSWs and LPs:

'They [LPs] need a bit more time when they join. I try to give more time at the outset – think about will the other lads accept them? I try to get to know them, bring them out of their shell a bit, they're often very suspicious of anyone. Some immediately settle and find their niche. [Ours] was the first shop to have them. When one was here for 18 months and another a year, it's quite a wrench when they leave. Nine to four-thirty is a lot of hours. We are really short of volunteer hours if there is a gap [between placements].'

(Manager J, Oxford)

The need to work as part of an existing (and often daily-changing) team, along with the relative discipline of a shop/work environment, factors that are advantageous for some CSWs and LPs, can be dis-advantageous to the smooth working of the charity shop, depending upon the attitudes of all involved. Volunteers can resist the imposition of outsiders who might change the sense of identity and atmosphere of the back room of the shop in particular. 'We don't use Community Service Workers – outsiders are not always accepted easily' (Manager U, Oxford). Those on placements may themselves resist the compulsion to work or take orders:

'I don't think the scheme [probation CSW] works, frankly. We had one older man and he was brilliant, he worked and worked. The youngsters are nice but they are not enthusiastic workers. One girl wouldn't do anything. One was a lovely lad, but he just sat drawing all day. It needs more supervision.'

(Manager Z, Oxford)

Needless to say, not all placements are a success. One manager reported other volunteers experiencing a sense of intimidation when four LPs worked on a single placement, and some CSWs are recalled:

'I caught one youngster taking out of the till ... I was terrified when the warders came to recover him, handcuffs jangling ... but it got back to jail that I was tough. I've only got to ring – the phone is my weapon. Older men are better – it's too petty crime for them to take from charity.'

(Manager Q, Oxford)

The Oxford study demonstrates widespread support for the value of LPs by charity shop managers, even though all participating shops had had one prisoner recalled at some point. This support is largely due to the number of hours given per week over a relatively long period of time, but also because of the positive attitude that the majority bring to the work. The benefits to the charity shop are clearly less apparent in the case of probationer CSWs, often because of their poor attitude and unreliability. This distinction is explained by one probation officer: 'People in jail want to get out for five days, whereas community service workers don't want to [be here] – they're all excuses' (Probation Officer 1, Oxfordshire Probation Service, recently retired).

Significantly, similar problems were reported where New Deal placements had been initiated, whereby some of those those on Job Seeker's (unemployment) benefit are required to undertake voluntary work. However, many managers persist in working with community service placements and those undertaking voluntary work in order to qualify for their Job Seeker's Allowance, because of the obvious benefits where these 'volunteers' are willing to contribute rather than fulfilling the necessity of a binding order – that is, where the individual chooses to work within the structural constraints in which they find themselves. This is achieved where their own sense of affiliation and sociation is enhanced, through identification with the mission of the charity and acceptance/appreciation of their contribution to the charity, in addition to the benefits of training and/or rehabilitation into society. This makes for a complex set of social relations within the space of the charity shop and between the shop and its locality, as well as the wider voluntary sector and the state.

The use of these different types of volunteers and CSWs illustrates that volunteers of all types represent the reciprocal nature of the relationship between charity shops and the local communities where they are located, with charity shops both providing and benefiting from a service beyond their strict remit (Maddrell 2000). However, by taking volunteers from this wider pool, charity shops are also taking on greater risks and difficulties *vis-à-vis* training and the need for professionalised operations that require at least some staff to be familiar with charity policy, legal requirements and retail technology. This has resulted in the often creative but potentially fraught combination of paid staff, traditional volunteers, school pupils, referred volunteers and those obliged to complete CSOs. All of this in turn requires greater management of staff – the often unseen cost of using volunteers.

Paid staff

The most widespread and far-reaching change in terms of charity shop staffing has been the introduction of paid managers at shop level. Early studies showed that the majority of paid staff worked at regional or head office level, with responsibility for policy formulation and implementation (Horne and Broadbridge 1994). By the late 1990s the majority of charity shops were headed by paid managers, usually with previous retail management experience, reflecting the move by many charity shops into the retail mainstream (Phelan 1997). However, while 65 per cent of shops in the sector are headed by a full-time paid manager (Phelan 1999a), it is still possible to find voluntary managers within the most 'professional' of charity chains. Oxfam is the most notable example: only 16 per cent of its 847 shops are under a paid manager (see Table 5.2). Indeed, excluding Oxfam, 73 per cent of outlets belonging to the largest charity chains employ paid managers (Phelan 1999), with many charities making this a matter of policy, resulting in 100 per cent of shops being under paid managers – for

Table 5.2 Paid staff in charity shops

Charity	Shops with paid manager (%)	Wage bill as percentage of turnover
Oxfam	16	—
British Heart Foundation	100	—
ICRF	77	17.6
Help the Aged	100	42.0
SCOPE	100	31.0
Barnardo's	96	33.5
Cancer Research Campaign	98	22.7
British Red Cross	75	—
Sue Ryder	—	—
Age Concern	84	29.1
National Trust	100	21.2
Cards for Good Causes	7	—
Royal Society for the Protection of Birds	92	14.1
St Peter's Hospice Bristol	95	—
Trinity Hospice Shops	100	22
St Giles Hospice Shops	91	21

Source: Phelan (1999)

example the British Heart Foundation, Help the Aged, SCOPE, Shelter and the NSPCC (National Society for the Prevention of Cruelty to Children).

A response in part to the competition for volunteers and in part to a professionalising sector, the introduction of paid managers has had a number of advantages. Notably it ensures the full-time presence of the manager on the shop premises, allowing for the consistent application of the charity's retail policy, for example on pricing, display and customer relations as well as supervision of volunteers. All these developments are particularly important to those charities seeking to establish formal top-down management of their retailing operations, with head office directives playing an increasingly important role in defining retail practice. In contrast, volunteer managers are much more hands-off, often being absent for three-quarters of the trading week (Broadbridge and Horne 1996). Such prolonged absence has many implications for the autonomy and responsibility of volunteers in the shop, but evidence suggests that volunteer-managed shops often have long-standing (if older) staff, allowing for greater continuity of practice (Whithear 1999).

The introduction of paid managers (sometimes coupled with paid assistant managers) has brought its own pressures to the operations of charity shops. This can be seen in a number of ways. For example, there may be tensions if managers from a mainstream retailing background introduce more formalised practices to long-standing volunteers. The necessity to recoup the salaries of paid staff from shop profits also creates an immediate need to increase turnover and net profits before actual income from the shop to the charity can grow. The same applies to clusters of charity shops reporting to a paid area or regional manager, whose salary will be offset from their region's shops' income.

Although remuneration is far from generous (declared salaries for full-time mangers ranged between £5,900 and £15,000 (Phelan 1999b)), Phelan's (ibid.) comparison of salaries for a sample of 16 large or medium-sized charity chains showed wages increasing from 22 per cent to 28 per cent of turnover between 1995 and 1999, resulting in a decline in surplus. Another comparison of charity shop wage bills[6] indicated a 16.8 per cent increase from £40 million to £46.8 million, attributable to an increased number of shops in some cases, such as that of the British Heart Foundation, but largely the result of increased salaries and a larger paid workforce (predicted by Mintel (1997)). Evidence from the largest charity retailers suggests that increased gross sales have been achieved by the introduction of professional staff, and there is a positive relationship between wages and profitability generally (although not a particularly 'robust' one), and there are exceptions, notably the hospice sector, where there is no correlation between the two (Phelan 1997: 20).

The introduction of weekly and monthly turnover and income targets set by (paid) area or regional managers has given some staff a sense of motivation and achievement, as noted by Whithear (1999). However, the pressure and accompanying changes in shop policy on pricing and turnover of goods have proved onerous to some volunteers (Phelan 1997) and served to alienate other volunteer staff:

> 'We have very good customers and very good turnover [more than trebled since the introduction of the paid manager] . . . but volunteers don't like the pressure I put them under, like reliability and rules from head office, like no eating or sitting at the till and no chatting – only to customers.'
>
> (Manager Q, Oxford)

This reflects the tensions in a professionalising sector where professionalisation is seen as being founded on greater use of qualified professionals and the consequent application of business practices to the charity sector (see Goodall 2000c), usually with the aim of max-imising profits.

However, the extent of the introduction of paid managers (and 'professional' practices) varies, reflecting the complexity of the sector, with diversity in practice both between and cutting across charities and areas. For example, in the Oxford study, thirteen of the seventeen (76 per cent) charity shops were run by paid managers (1998), with two of the three unpaid managers running shops belonging to large charity chains. Local-initiative 'organic' charity shops are often com-pletely run by volunteers, but some, such as hospice shops in large towns, may have paid managers, reflecting turnover. (Ninety to a hundred per cent of outlets in the top ten hospice chains or shops (by turnover) have paid managers (Phelan 1999).) In turn, small-town shops may be run entirely by volunteers regardless of the size of the chain. For example, in the Isle of Man only two of fifteen shop man-agers interviewed were paid, even though more than half of the shops represent large national charity chains.

Assistant managers are commonly employed to cover the manager's day off, but their employment status can vary from a pro rata part-time salary to a £5 per day honorarium, depending on the shop. Other paid staff in the sector include those such as the PDSA's 'cus-tomer care assistant' with primary responsibility for front-of-shop activities, including security, freeing the manager to undertake train-ing activities for other staff, volunteer recruitment, book-keeping and other back-room activities.

Some charities, such as the Shaw Trust, have advertised for paid shop assistants (a policy necessitated by a shortage of volunteers in areas of high or 'full' employment), and charities dependent upon door-to-door collection of donated goods are increasingly having to employ part-time van drivers. Volunteers remain the main source of staffing hours in the overwhelming majority of charity shops, but these volunteers, like the charity shops themselves, have become a more heterogeneous group rather than comprising solely what might be described as the 'traditional volunteer' associated with the sector. Charity shop managers are likely to have to become increasingly creat-ive in their recruitment and matching of volunteers to tasks, including the use of flexible (i.e. non-shop opening) hours and regular episodic opportunities for volunteers, to accommodate those in paid work. They will also have to provide support and training to other volunteers who need these. It may be possible for episodic volunteers with pro-fessional skills to provide some of the necessary training and support, but all of this will require co-ordination and creative management.

Notes

1 These approaches include (i) the 'opportunity cost' of volunteer time, (ii) the 'replacement cost' and (iii) the 'output-based' approach (V. Foster 1997) and the Volunteer Investment and Value Audit (VIVA). Each method of assigning value to volunteer work has its own limitations: the assumption that volunteers choose between volunteering and paid work, differential wage rates, and awareness of the benefits that volunteers accrue through their voluntary work. VIVA is the only method to incorporate the financial costs incurred by charities deploying and managing volunteers (ibid.), but understanding these costs is vital to evaluating volunteer input.

2 Studies of volunteers in Aids-related charities in the USA suggest that collective identification based on sexuality appears to be important in patterns of male homosexual volunteering (Simon *et al.* 2000).

3 See Kenwright (2000) on projects in the Women's Refuge in York.

4 Responses from male volunteers in the Oxford and Isle of Man studies were combined to give greater statistical relevance.

5 This is based on Maddrell's study of volunteers in Oxford, including a particular study of community service workers and licensed prisoners.

6 For the twenty-two charities providing details of wage bills in 1998 and 1999.

6 Pricing and competition
Hitting the mark

While it is generally assumed that exchange is about creating equival-ence and commensurability, the sale of goods in 'alternative' markets cuts across this assumption. On the basis of the apparently contradict-ory studies by Clarke (2000) on parent sales of baby clothes and Gregson *et al.*'s (2000) on clothing in charity shops, Miller argues that exchange here appears as 'a process of making objects appropri-ate to those involved in the exchange itself, and operates primarily through bringing together rather than separating the abstract and the particular' (Miller 2000: 79).

Most charity shop customers are 'looking for a bargain', a bargain being an item having a high perceived value to the customer and being sold/bought at a low price. Customers may go bargain-hunting for reasons of necessity, thrift or fun, or as a result of a more subcon-scious desire to 'experience shopping as saving', as suggested by Miller (1998). The low price is relative to the perceptions of the customer. Price from the customer's viewpoint can be described as Price = Qual-ity/Value. Price is therefore the payment for quality as interpreted by the valuation of the marketplace (Hanna and Dodge 1995).The sell-ing or retail price of goods in conventional retailing is set so as to satisfy the needs and wants of the customer, to act as a competitive tool against the competitor and, when goods are sold, to generate a profit. Goods and services are usually sold at prices that are higher than production cost, allowing for the retail costs to be covered and passed on to the consumer. Determining the retail price requires detailed systems in most cases, which take into consideration such factors as location, competition, the nature of the merchandise and the character of the customer. In most retail sectors, therefore, pricing decisions are regarded as being the most crucial as well as the most difficult aspect of retail marketing. The importance and the com-plexity of this function show enormous variation between different sectors and types of retailing, including the charity shop sector. While price could be considered to be unimportant in the marketing strategy of a non-profit organisation, the provision of a subsidised service (a category into which charity shops might fall) involves making strategic marketing decisions of the kind that must be made by any profit-making organisation (Hannagan 1992).

The charity shop experience is that of purchasing goods at bargain prices. Customer valuation of these second-cycle consumption goods is therefore inverted in terms of conventional retailing, when a high price will often reflect the 'value' nature of the goods. In the case of the charity shop, where goods are donated with no purchase cost, it could be argued that the pricing of these goods is not difficult. It might also be suggested that if the charity shop is deemed to have a primary or secondary function in providing a service to a local community, then the prices set should be determined at whatever level the customer can pay and could maximally afford. However, if the reason for the charity shop is to maximise its fund-raising capability (generally the primary, if not the sole, purpose), then a careful retail pricing strategy has to be in place.

Until a few years ago, pricing strategies in retailing received very little attention, and the importance of pricing as a function of the marketing mix was not fully appreciated. Two studies were conducted in 1986, when commercial retailer managers in Europe and the USA were asked to rank the importance of certain marketing areas. The results showed pricing to be the most important (Simon 1989). By contrast, in a similar study conducted about twenty years earlier, pricing was ranked only sixth in importance. This change reflects the growing awareness of the significance of pricing a product or service, which is, as Monroe (1979), has argued, one of the most vital decisions that can be made, since price is the only marketing variable that generates income. Despite this, however, the role of price has been minimal or even omitted in some recent studies of consumption (e.g. Mort 1996). Given the level and the amount of competition faced by charity shops, from both other charity shops and traditional retailers, it has become vitally important for them to examine their marketing strategy, and in particular their pricing strategy.

If the purpose of charity shop sales is to generate sufficient revenue to cover the costs and produce a surplus for the benefit of the charity, then traditional ideas about pricing strategy must change (Octon 1983). Bruce (1998) suggests that the definitions of the four Ps of the marketing mix – Product, Price, Place and Promotion – were constructed with no reference to the fund-raising activities of voluntary organisations.

It is certainly true that traditional retail pricing policies and strategies are aimed almost exclusively at new goods, taking into account important factors such as cost price, distribution costs, staff costs, rent, taxes and competition – which often have little relevance for donated goods. It is clear that since these factors are not always relevant to charity shops, traditional retail pricing policies and strategies might not always be applicable.

Pricing objectives: what charities hope to achieve

The objectives that tend to underlie most retail pricing decisions are those of long-term profit maximisation, short-term profit maximisation, market penetration, market defence, market stabilisation, quality image, pricing integrity and run-down pricing. These objectives form the basis for pricing policies, but are not necessarily mutually exclusive – a retailer might pursue different objectives at different times or in different outlets (McGoldrick 1990). It is at this point in the pricing process that the charity retailer has to decide 'what business we are in'. For example, is the shop portraying a quality image in order to maximise long-term profit and should therefore charge 'realistic' prices in market terms, or is it providing a service to a low-income neighbourhood and should therefore price according to its customers' means? The retail model described as the Wheel of Retailing demonstrates how the trading up in assortment quality and service has led to higher prices being charged for goods (Horne 2000).

Once the overall objectives are determined, the pricing policy can be set. For an effective policy to be put in place it is necessary to select an appropriate target market, which will in turn determine the retail image (Berman and Evans 1995). The retailer has then to decide on a broad pricing policy along the lines either that no competitors will have lower prices or higher prices, or alternatively that prices will be consistent with competitors'. It might be that all items would be priced individually depending on the demand for each and that the prices for all items be interrelated in order to maintain an image and to ensure that a reasonable profit is returned. Price leadership could be exerted, for example, or prices could remain constant throughout the year or change as merchandise changes. Once the broad pricing policy has been determined, specific pricing policies can then be decided. These could include market penetration pricing, market skimming pricing, perceived value pricing and price discrimination (Doyle 1991).

Where *market penetration pricing* is used, short-term profits are sacrificed by setting prices at a low level in order to gain a large share of the market. Some theoreticians, for example Winkler (1983), advise against this policy unless it is absolutely certain that existing competition is unable to undercut prices.

Market skimming involves setting high initial prices in order to achieve high profit margins over a relatively small volume in the short term. According to Doyle, this policy is viable when a segment of consumers of significant size exists which will buy at the high initial price. It can also be used when the organisation has limited resources with which to expand, or when the high initial price will not attract an immediate competitive take-over of the market. It is also viable when the high prices create an image of a superior product. It is therefore possible for a charity shop to operate a market skimming policy if it has limited production capacity and resources with which to expand. Most of the charities researched automatically mark down the prices of articles if they have not been sold after a certain period of time, usually two to four weeks. Mark-downs are price reductions that are implemented at certain times of the year, or even at certain times of the day, to allow old stock to be sold off, thus maintaining 'clean stock' levels. They create room for new stock to be brought to the front of shop and thereby foster customer goodwill (Cox and Brittain 1988).

The majority of charity shops operate a system of circulating donated goods, using codes to identify the week in which stock was introduced to the shop floor. It is common practice that after two to four weeks these goods are then reduced in price or removed, either for recirculating or for ragging (see Chapter 4). Regular customers get to know the system of particular shops and operate their purchasing decisions in relation to this, especially where they have established a relationship with the managers (see Chapter 3):

> 'Regulars come in and say, "What have you got reduced today, Maureen?" They know the system: after three weeks, clothes are reduced to half-price; they look at the ticket and say, "This is on its third week, Maureen". They try to haggle but I only allow reductions when they go on the £1 rail outside.'
>
> (Manager O, Oxford)

Many retailers operate an automatic mark-down plan, whereby the amount and timing of mark-downs are controlled by the length of time the merchandise remains in stock. Alternatively, retailers hold a store-wide clearance, which usually takes place once or twice a year, the aim being to clear out merchandise before beginning the next season. The advantages of this system over the automatic mark-down plan are that merchandise can be offered, and potentially sold, at the original price for a longer period of time, and that clearance sales limit bargain hunting to once or twice a year. Automatic mark-downs, on the other hand, encourage a steady flow of bargain-hunters with the 'Why buy now when it will be on sale next week?' attitude (Berman and Evans 1995). Such an attitude is particularly relevant to charity shop retailing, where bargain hunting is the norm.

The majority of charity shops hold sales at some time in the year. Most hold clearance sales twice-yearly to clear stock in preparation for the next season. The others leave it to the judgement of individual shop managers to decide if and when to hold a 'one-off' sale. One charity said:

> 'We tend to do one-off sales but we don't have them as a regular thing because we find that people tend to wait, knowing that certain items in the shops will then be reduced and they will get to know what you are going to do and they will wait for you.'
>
> (Manager, Scotland)

And:

> 'We generally go with the flow and reduce prices if sales are low ... if we have a surplus of stock we try half-price sales before we rag off the glut'.
>
> (Manager V, Oxford)

Perceived value pricing bases price on the buyer's perception of the value of a product relative to that of the competition. In the case of charity shops, the competition could mean goods from other charity shops or similar new goods purchased from a traditional retail outlet. Value has a diversity of meanings but is principally seen as a twofold indicator. It gives an item's use in relation to market variables such as price and equivalence, but it is also the more personal attribute of indicating what really matters to an individual – that is, what can't be attributed to the market. However, most people's exercise of sense of value in practice transcends and omits the dualism of the characteristics of market and gift (Miller 2000). Anthropological work suggests that value is created by the act of exchange, with the implication that the value of an item is defined according to the varying context of transaction (ibid.) – hence in terms of second and subsequent cycles of consumption, the next stage in a material good's life history might be determined by the location of its resale. For example, a second-hand painting might be deemed desirable if it were sold in Sotheby's, simply for that reason, but perhaps ignored if it were presented for sale in a charity shop. The extent to which culture influences the concept of value is hotly debated. Miller (2000: 79) suggests that rather than culture being the supposed context or constraint on commerce, 'commerce is often itself the force and infrastructure which is used to create culture as normativity' – that is, culture can be seen as a product of commerce rather than vice versa. This (often unconscious) working out/out-working of value has significant impact on the attribution of value to goods for resale within a charity shop.

McGoldrick (1990) suggests that any pricing decision must be taken with regard to the pricing position of competitors. However, although it is important constantly to review the prices of competitors' goods, it is ultimately the customers' subjective impressions of competitors' prices that are essential when making pricing decisions. Nearest competitors, either other charity shops or local discount shops, often influence prices, with a number of charity shop managers admitting to monitoring prices in other charity shops and then undercutting these. 'Our prices are the cheapest in town' (Manager K, Isle of Man). When retailers base their prices on those charged by their competitors, *competitor-oriented pricing* is in operation. Where this kind of strategy is used, the retailer might not alter its prices to react to changes in demand or costs unless competitors alter theirs. Furthermore, rival charity shops are more likely to cut the prices of their own goods in reaction to mark-downs (which could potentially initiate a price war) than to have seasonal clearances. This would be particularly dangerous for charity shops, as according to Golden and Zimmerman (1986), 'It is wise to avoid pricing practices that would lead to price wars, but this is especially true for small operators.' Ali (1996: 48) agrees: 'as with retailers . . . so too with charities, price cutting can be dangerous'.

Another demand-based pricing policy is that of *price discrimination*. Here different types of customer are charged different prices for similar products. It is perhaps most common in a geographical context. Howe (1992) argues that deviations from national price levels should be considered where there are regional differences in consumers' income levels and local retail competitors. For example, the local market within which a retail store of a multiple chain operates is different from that experienced by every other store in the chain, and therefore most multiple retailers will differentiate some or all of their prices accordingly. However, in the case of some discount chains, rigid pricing policies are enforced across every store in the group since they consider that their prices are competitive in any location (McGoldrick 1990).

The majority of the charities researched confirmed that their prices vary according to the geographical location of their shops between and within regions. This suggests a policy of geographical price discrimination, which can include raising as well as reducing prices:

'We follow headquarters guidelines, but we have slight flexibility. Actually we put up all the prices by one grade, because of the area. Nearly all our clothes are designer labels; we need a whole range of prices to cope with all those goods.'

(Manager N, Oxford)

Variation in prices within charity shop multiples also occurs where circulation chains are used – that is, where goods such as women's clothing are provided in bulk to shop A, with the requirement to pass on the same number of garments to shop B, the next shop in the chain. Goods offered at the end of the chain are often heavily discounted, for example in the Oxfam Supersaver Shops, which are typically located in less affluent areas.

Other pricing policies particularly relevant to charity shops are those of declared versus negotiated pricing, price lining and moral pricing. *Declared versus negotiated pricing* is also known as fixed/flexible pricing. According to Gabor (1977), those retailers that price-mark each individual article or display the price of the article separately, and do not permit any deviation from the stated price, operate a policy of declared pricing. On the other hand, some retailers may operate a policy of negotiated pricing where, for example, there is considerable scope for a retailer to charge different prices to different types of customer or at different times of the day or days of the week, for example on 'pensioners' day'. Some charity shops were found to have notices written on the till stating that 'The prices marked on our garments are fixed. Please do not ask for reductions' (shop P, Oxford), with the result that few shoppers try to haggle. However, more generally, it is not possible to monitor whether headquarters policy on pricing is strictly adhered to at all times, and given the nature of charity shop retailing, it is quite probable that some bartering does occur:

'We have the usual little lot [of customers who haggle], but we're willing to drop the prices with those we know can't afford much.'

(Manager L, Isle of Man)

'It is not possible to monitor if this policy of non-negotiable pricing is strictly adhered to in each individual shop. We have a basic price list, but if volunteers think it should be more or less, they will alter the price.'

(Manager L, Isle of Man)

Managers are least likely to allow haggling or reductions on their best-quality merchandise, particularly collectables or designer label clothes, as one manager protested: 'She just asked me to reduce those shoes from £3.00 – they're Van Dal, they're brand new' (Manager Q, Oxford).

While isolated cases of bartering do occur, especially with dealers and well-known customers and those for whom price negotiation is part of the buzz of charity shop consumption, clearly the more 'professional' charities operate a policy of declared pricing as opposed to a policy of negotiated pricing. Other shops, however, operate a more flexible approach to pricing particular items to individuals or groups of people:

'We're not supposed to barter, but we're also supposed to reject old-fashioned clothes, but I put out crimplene dresses at low prices and shirts with $16^{1}/_{2}$ collar size for older men at £1.50 – what those who are in need are looking for.'

(Manager Q, Oxford)

The policy of *price lining* is based on the principle of selling goods at a limited range of price points, each of which represents a distinct level of quality (Berman and Evans 1995). Harper (1966) suggests that retailers that practise price lining should limit their stock to two or three price categories which reflect the 'good', 'better' and 'best' of each kind of merchandise. Price lines are usually selected on the basis of past experience with the prices at which most sales of the products are made.

The advantage of price lining is that the pricing task for a retailer is simplified. Once the price lines are chosen, the retailer has only to select the merchandise that is appropriate for each price line, which simplifies inventory control and customers' buying decisions. Price lining also helps retailers to avoid frequent price changes, which in turn reduces the possibility of price wars. From interviews with fourteen of the top twenty retail charities it was concluded that most charities operate a policy of price lining, since the majority of the charities that were interviewed compile price guides for their shops that are based on a series of quality levels. For example, one charity has four price bands, which respectively represent the very minimum, low quality, medium quality and high quality, making it easy for the shop manager or pricing team to apply the appropriate prices once the level of quality of each item has been decided.

Winkler (1983) suggests that *moral pricing* is based on a notion of justice and fairness, and is principally used by those organisations where costs are particularly difficult to identify or where the subject may be socially or politically sensitive. This relates to the broader mission of many charities. It supports, for example, those aiming to serve the local needy, such as the Salvation Army or charities supporting the aged. They prioritise accessible pricing over the maximisation of turnover and profit (Manager U, Oxford), perhaps by offering a discount each day for a particular target group, such as pensioners. 'Every Thursday we have half-price clothes for pensioners' (Manager R, Oxford). This could be seen as democratisation of consumption via pricing (as indeed could be said of the charity shop sector as a whole), but charity shop managers tend to be pragmatic about the range of goods they 'democratise' in this way: 'Sometimes we have to take the very best things out the back, otherwise the best stuff goes and we lose the income' (Manager R, Oxford).

There are anomalies in the approach to pricing goods in charity shops: one charity interviewed in a Scottish study operated a fixed price policy, with all goods on sale for the seemingly low price of 50p or less. Although the charity wants to make money, it also sees some of its inner-city shops as offering a service to the community and therefore operates a pricing policy in accordance with that perceived objective, in effect operating as a discount charity shop. Even selling at these very low prices, the shops operate at a profit. However, this policy can evoke problems with the donors of goods to the shops, who were not happy with their goods being sold at 'these ridiculously low prices'.

It is suggested that the value of clothes in charity shops is intrinsically linked to their previous use, particularly for middle-class consumers (see Miller 2000: 80). While clearly the case in antique, collectable or retro fashions, all of which will be valued (in both senses) in large part because of their authenticity (and arguably the known provenance is part of the construct of value in the case of baby clothes, as Clarke (2000) suggests), this applies only to this minority element of the charity shop offering. The majority of second-hand clothes *rely* upon decontextualising (see Chapter 3 and Gregson *et al.* 2000), drawing on the brand label only for context, if applicable.

Pricing strategies

Once a pricing policy or combination of policies has been selected, the retailer then has to choose a pricing strategy, which determines how prices are to be set on a regular basis. These typically include *demand-oriented pricing*, which determines the range of prices acceptable to the target market. Retailers can set demand-based prices according to the type of customer, type of product, location of outlet or time of purchase (Cox and Brittain, 1988). One particular feature of demand-oriented pricing is the price–quality association. This is a concept which states that many consumers believe that high prices connote high quality and low prices connote low quality, and therefore will not buy a product if they consider the price to be too high or too low (Berman and Evans 1995). Within the charity shop, value is not just about the dualism of exchange and personal value, but also about 'value for money' or turning money into value – in ways not possible within first-cycle consumption. Just as increasing the value of an item can be achieved by the processes of cleaning and re-presenting before sale, so Miller (2000: 81) suggests that second-hand/second-cycle consumption is based on the intention to 'make the clothes into objects that we come to value in every sense of that term'. As Gregson *et al.* (2000) demonstrate, cleaning is at the heart of the creation of value in charity shops, being a process that negotiates notions of acceptability in terms of retail practice and personal standards, as well as associated perceptions of consumers' identity.

In the charity shop arena there is an added complication, that of the retail volunteer. Their concept of the worth of goods is also pertinent to the pricing strategy. Where goods are priced by a range of staff, including volunteers, they can become rather *ad hoc*. Where this has occurred, there is often some degree of rationalisation, for example by the strict application of headquarters pricing guidelines or limiting this task to managers and assistant managers. However, even this strategy can be fraught: 'I priced this designer mac at £50; after my day off she [the assistant manager] had reduced it to £10. I had to change it again' (Manager O, Oxford).

Within charity shops, demand can be quite elastic. Consumers motivated by the desire for a bargain are often prepared to forgo a purchase if the price is not right. As one recently appointed manager attested,

'The previous manager had a policy of low prices to make a quick profit, with a 50p and a £2 rail for clean, basic stuff. I tried to increase the prices, but the clothes just sat on the rail. Sometimes the volunteers know what prices people will pay.'

(Manager R, Oxford)

Where volunteers are involved with pricing a large range of goods, their pricing can reflect their own interests and values, and specifically they can over-price their own donated goods, to which they retain some sense of attachment. Conversely, other goods may not be recognised as particularly valuable by a non-specialist; for example, retro fashion or collectables. Where volunteers are actively involved in pricing goods, some charities run briefing sessions highlighting high-value items. Specialist high-value goods such as cameras or jewellery are commonly priced by an expert volunteer or a supportive local shopkeeper.

Cost-oriented pricing occurs where organisations set prices largely on the basis of product costs. It includes mark-up pricing, cost-plus pricing and target pricing. It can be assumed at this stage, however, that in the case of donated goods, charity shops do not use cost-oriented pricing, although the growing practice of house-to-house bag collection necessitates pricing levels sufficient to cover collection costs. The cost of cleaning and re-presenting donated goods also has to be realistically covered.

A successful pricing strategy integrates all three concepts of demand, cost and competitor-oriented pricing (Cox and Brittain 1988). Since the merchandise is donated, it would seem likely that prices will be influenced by what the market is prepared to pay, and therefore that demand-oriented pricing will be favoured. Equally, as a result of the rise in the number of charity shops all competing for customers, coupled with the tendency for charity shops to 'cluster' in town centres, it would be fair to assume that competitor-oriented pricing is increasingly an element in pricing strategy.

According to James *et al.* (1981), retailers should also assess competitors' prices on identical and substitute merchandise. This information is necessary, since a price-level strategy should be related to the general prevailing level of prices. The decision by a retailer whether to set prices above, below or with the market is very important since this will ultimately affect its image as perceived by customers. James *et al.* (1981) suggest that retailers who use *above-the-market* pricing strategies usually price most or all of their merchandise at a price higher than the comparable merchandise of their competitors on the assumption that price is usually not a major concern to their customers. They suggest that features such as extensive assortments, exclusive offerings, or very fashionable merchandise and excellent supplementary services such as repairs or alterations make an above-the-market price strategy viable. Although not instantly recognisable as being applicable to charity shops, above-the-market pricing is used in some instances. For example, if the charity has a strong brand image or it sells very high-quality or fashionable items, it can sustain higher prices than the competition.

Some retailers, particularly smaller retailers, often price with the market because of the nature and type of products they sell. This may be because the merchandise that they sell is very similar or identical to that of competitors, and therefore price-sensitive consumers would quickly switch to whichever store had the lowest prices (Golden and Zimmerman 1986). James *et al.* (1981) suggest that this is the strategy adopted by the majority of retailers, and that these retailers choose to compete on non-price factors such as service and product assortment, which are harder for competitors to match than lower prices. Those charity shops selling a proportion of bought-in new goods find themselves in this situation, but price cutting in these circumstances may mean making a loss on the new goods, which in turn reduces profit maximisation.

Retailers wanting to price most of or all their offerings below the prevailing market level adopt the strategy of below-the-market pricing. It is suggested by James *et al.* that, given a few exceptions, if the firm is to profit, then low prices must be coupled with limited assortments, low operating expenses, fewer supplementary services and economical physical factors. This combination is termed discount pricing, low-margin retailing or simply discounting, which is what all charity shops do when pricing donated goods. It would seem logical that charity shops would be unable to price above the market, given the criteria that have to be met in order to do so. It is more likely therefore that charity shops will endeavour to set their prices either with or below the charity sector market, but, as illustrated, different practices are emerging.

Price decisions

Pricing policies and strategies are designed to guide and influence the pricing decisions. Who makes these decisions depends on the structure and philosophy of the individual organisation. In most retail organisations it is top-level management who decide the important pricing strategies and policies. In the charity sector, however, it is usually the local shop manager who takes the responsibility for most specific pricing decisions.

It is frequently the case that specific decisions are made in isolation. In many companies the pricing activities are dispersed between different parts of the organisation (McGoldrick 1990). For example, it is most common for the top management to determine the basic pricing philosophies but the retail managers to be responsible for specific price-setting decisions, a concept reflected in the charity shop sector. The rationale for this is that lower-level managers have a better understanding of the pricing policies of local competitors (Golden and Zimmerman 1986). Managers *in situ* have a much closer relationship with their customers and therefore understand how much they are willing to pay.

Almost two-thirds of the top retailing charities interviewed stated that pricing policies and strategies are set at head office and that national price guidelines are then issued to each retail outlet. Each shop manager, in some cases in liaison with area managers, is then responsible for pricing individual items according to the national guidelines. In most cases these guidelines are compiled and issued twice a year. Some charities expect guidelines to be strictly adhered to, wherever the shop is located:[1] 'You get the super-greedy [customer]; one man got a pair of new curtains for £2, then he wanted a tea towel and vase thrown in for the price' (Manager K, Isle of Man). Others, such as Shelter, take the view that individual shop managers are more likely to know the state of the local market. That view is substantiated further in that where shops are local initiatives – for example, hospice shops and/or those set up in short-term accommodation – the prices are usually determined *in situ*. The manager of a temporary shop in Liverpool stated:

> 'I can set prices myself. Other charities are very expensive; people come in and say that our prices are cheap (£1 for ordinary blouses, £3 for labels). I think charity shops are for people who can't afford to spend much money. [During the interview a customer requested a reduction on an item of clothing from £3.50. "Will you take £3?" "Yes." Reductions are still a sale, you still get £3 out of £3.50, but I don't allow reductions with the best stuff.'
>
> (Manager G, Liverpool)

As we have seen, the prices set in the more professional chains of charity shops are usually determined by set prices or guidelines from head office or regional headquarters, but many managers subvert what are considered to be inflexible price codes. Others have considerable autonomy. The variation and complexity of local pricing can be seen from the following quotations:

'Head office send a price guide, but each shop has its own prices, depending on its customers.'

(Manager T, Oxford)

'We have a pricing guideline, but it is done mostly by intuition . . . designer labels, "in" colours and condition denote price sometimes.'

(Manager Y, Oxford)

'There is a price booklet, but the prices are too high. I keep prices low and have a high turnover of stock.'

(Manager X, Oxford)

'We use the set prices; they're reasonably fair.'

(Manager H, Liverpool)

Seven main criteria have been identified (Slingsby 1997) as being used when setting prices of donated goods in fourteen of the largest charity retailers. These seven criteria are the quality of goods, the price as new, the label, the mode, the location of the charity shop, the local competition and the experience of the shop manager. As can be seen from Table 6.1, the most influential factors in determining price seem to be the quality of goods, the location of the shop, competition, the price of articles as new, and the label/brand name. Quality is the highest priority for donated goods, and the more professionalised charity shops will not sell any sub-standard or outmoded articles, preferring to rag sub-standard goods rather than risk selling them.

The majority of charities agree that their prices are affected to some extent by the location of their shops. Two of the top charities operate a certain number of shops in less affluent areas where lower prices are charged, but claim that their remaining shops should charge similar prices for similar-quality goods wherever they are located. The majority, however, admitted that the location of shops did influence their pricing quite dramatically. As one charity retail director said, 'national or regional price guides can go badly wrong because areas change from one mile to the next'. One charity that said that its prices are not affected by location claimed that the price of the article is determined by its quality alone:

Table 6.1 Criteria used to set prices

Charity	Quality of goods	Price as new	Label	Mode	Location	Competition
1	*	*	*	*		*
2	*	*	*	*		*
3	*	*	*	*	*	
4	*	*			*	*
5	*		*	*	*	*
6	*	*			*	*
7	*	*	*	*		*
8	*	*			*	*
9	*	*	*		*	*
10	*		*		*	*
11	*				*	*
12	*				*	*
13	*				*	
14	*				*	*
Total	14	8	7	5	11	12

Source: Adapted from Slingsby (1997)

'There is an interesting misconception . . . that the charity shop is there to supply cheap goods to the community. That is not the case. The charity shop is there to raise funds for its charity, and there is a subtle difference.'

This statement reinforces the concept of the charity shop in terms of its function or purpose. The entire operational focus pivots on whether its desire is primarily to serve its community or to raise funds for the charity.

Most of the charities that have a national pricing policy research the prices of high street retailers such as Marks & Spencer and then work out the average prices of items such as men's suits, ladies' dresses, ladies' blouses. They then calculate a percentage of between 10 and 25 per cent of the average price, and this figure is used to compile price 'bands'. The specific number of bands varies between charities, but they all have between three and five. It was found that all those charities that research the prices of high street retailers have more than one hundred shops, which might suggest a greater deal of professionalism. The charities that do not research high street prices seem to base their own prices almost exclusively on the three factors of quality, competition and location of the shop, suggesting the use of a combination of demand-oriented and competitor-oriented pricing.

There is little evidence of the existence of price competition between the majority of charity shops, but nearest competitors, either other charity shops or local discount shops, often influence prices, with a number of managers admitting to monitoring prices in other charity shops and then undercutting them. The majority of charities claim to review the prices of their competitors on a regular basis; however, they generally do so in an attempt to make sure that they are pricing 'with the market' rather than to undercut competitors' prices. Two of the largest charity shop chains do try to set their prices above those of their competitors, but it was concluded that this is more of a statement of quality within the charity shop market. Three different charity shops in Oxford claim to be the 'Harrods' of the charity shop sector! None of these charities reacts to sudden price changes made by their competitors. Only one charity admitted that it tries to make sure that its prices are the lowest possible at all times. It can be concluded, therefore, that a small minority of charity shops set their prices either above or below the market while the majority 'play safe' and price with the market.

Pricing in charity shops is not an exact science but rather the result of a complex interaction of charity-specific factors. Customers in different locations have particular perceptions of acceptable price levels and will not pay more than that perceived level. Pricing strategies allow price to be based on a percentage of the '*original price*' or perceived value of the goods, but shop location and local environment make it difficult for charities running more than one shop to have a consistent pricing policy. 'The pricing of donated second-hand goods is "very fickle"; something is only worth what someone is prepared to pay' (Regional Manager Charity X). A garment's average price can be determined relative to high street prices, but ultimately the policy has to be to get as much money as possible in a particular outlet. Although this is the reality of pricing policy, those charity retailers wishing to maximise their fund-raising potential are those with the thought-through pricing policies, whereas those charity shops selling low-cost goods as a service to the community tend to be those making price decisions on the shop floor.

Price is a particularly important factor affecting demand for comparative goods. Many consumers using charity shops treat donated goods as comparative goods and indeed are encouraged to do so by the clustering of charity shops, despite the uniqueness of products on sale. Thus demand can be very price elastic. Miller suggests that housewives' (*sic*) knowledge of comparative pricing is an important component of the moral economy of their household purchases, 'as well as an important element of rivalry and status competition between house-wives' (1995b: 37). Similarly, finding the 'best prices' and getting particularly good bargains has become part of the culture of and rivalry between committed charity shop consumers. Asked what would encourage them to use charity shops, more than 36 per cent of high street shopper respondents in Oxford identified lower prices. Fifty-seven per cent of volunteer respondents and 51 per cent of shopper respondents also suggested that the provision of low-priced goods was the main value of charity shops in their immediate local community, suggesting that pricing is also crucial to the maintenance of good-will between the charity shop and potential customers, donors and volunteers in its locality. The apparent stagnation of the charity shop sector in 2000 has caused major charity retailers to review their pricing policy within a wider review of marketing strategy. Pricing has been crucial in attracting charity shop customers and will be central to maintaining demand for second-cycle consumption of donated goods.

Note

1 One large national charity chain reduced its rigid pricing policy in 2000 in response to decreasing profits, allowing local managers greater discretion and initiative.

7 'It's all in the mix'

Profits, life cycles, lifestyles and the future of charity shops

It can be seen from the previous chapters that to refer to 'charity shops' as indicative of a whole sector is as problematic as generalising about 'clothes shops' or 'food stores'. As the charity retail sector has developed, so the continuum of types has stretched in terms of store size, store function, the merchandise mix and the retail structure, with some charities operating a nation-wide chain of stores and others a single autonomous retail unit. One end of the scale shows charity shops with unrivalled retail professionalism, with shops at the opposite end primarily offering goods as a safety net for the socially excluded in society (although it has to be said that the majority of charity shops can be found in the middle ground, blending these functions). The corollary is a varied customer base, with consumption in charity shops being influenced by a complex overlapping and interfacing of motives, influences and desires on the part of shoppers, including thrift, economic necessity and lifestyle. Lifestyle can influence not only individual consumption choice, but also social interaction and even the creation of social networks in and through the space of charity shops in specific locations. Needless to say, these influences are circulating and reciprocal, with lifestyle in turn potentially being influenced by individuals' social experience of the charity shop. This chapter draws together these different functions of, and experiences within, charity shops, looking to their future as retail, consumption and social spaces.

The charity shop as social space

All charity shops function as social spaces. They are use spaces that generate interaction between shoppers, donors, volunteers and managers, but can also become meeting places, places of identification and sociation. The physical space or locale of the shop can also be divided functionally, with implications for the social relations associated with particular sub-spaces. The most explicit division is between the front and back of shop, the back being the hidden, limited-access 'dirty' space of sorting and cleaning donated goods, compared to the public, 'clean' shop floor where goods are presented and purchased. This dualism has been particularly associated with bodily functions, as with Goffman's front/back dichotomy (Gregson *et al.* 2000), an association that seems to be borne out in the case of those volunteers who reject back-room work and especially the sorting of donated goods, perceiving a risk of confronting dirt, disease and death. This negative association seems to be further reinforced by the fact that those doing community service hours under court order often prefer to stay in the back room (see Chapter 5), implying shady associations and a link with punishment and hard labour. However, the preference of many licensed prisoners to work in the public arena of the front of shop transgresses this simplistic dichotomy, as does the number of 'regular' volunteers also opting for the dirty (but possibly thrilling) work of sorting and cleaning unpredictable donated goods.

The charity shop can also constitute a space of performance. This can include the performance associated with browsing and the trying on of clothing (Gregson and Crewe 1998) typical of all forms of shopping but possibly liberated in the low-cost/low-risk arena of the charity shop. The character of the charity shop might also engender the performance of negotiation over price, in a manner not generally found in mainstream retailing, with dealers or those shoppers simply possessing the 'front' to try to push the boundaries of pricing policy. The bureaucratic space of the charity shop is embodied in the manager's office (if it exists) but is also represented materially in subdivisions of use space and manifested in regulations governing practices. Although regulations also operate in the front of shop, they are more often materialised in posters and lists of regulations in the back room. Where a hierarchical management structure is employed, then power relations will be centred on the person of the manager and her/his representatives, this performance of power relations moving within the shop at will. However, as was seen in the case of volunteers (and indeed managers) who were reluctant to abide by headquarters' regulations, charity shops can also be a site of resistance where rules are subverted and hierarchies of power undermined by small acts of autonomy and resistance.

There is also the performance of particular stages in life careers enacted through the space of the charity shop, whether as professional retailers/managers or as voluntary workers, each adding to their public persona through their work in the charity shop. A further performance is that of identity creation/reinforcement primarily through volunteering and consumption practices. Volunteers consciously or unconsciously reinforce their sense of identity as a caring, altruistic and/or hard-working person. In the case of shoppers, identity is largely reinforced through the purchase of identity signifiers, whether of individuality or of sociation. The identities constructed in part by the consumption of charity shop goods can be extremely varied, reflecting lifestyle choices. Some customers wish to subscribe to mainstream signifiers of material culture such as leading brands, whereas others seek a more specific/individualised image. Yet others choose to negate mainstream retail values, opting for ethical reasons to buy second-hand or fair trade goods.

A sense of sociation can also occur between volunteers identifying with one another and the charitable cause, or between shoppers and staff. It is here that we see a particular overlap with the social space of the locale or use space of the charity shop *qua* retail outlet, with the wider social relations of the surrounding locality. In growing out of (in the case of 'organic' shops) or becoming part of local social networks, charity shops both create and are influenced by existing social networks in their locality. Although friend-to-friend recruitment of volunteers has been shown to homogenise the volunteer base, it is effective and serves to reinforce local social networks. On the negative side it can work to exclude people who are not members of existing networks; on the positive side it can facilitate the embedding of a charity shop within broader local networks, for example when a shop manager gives a talk to the Women's Institute or a local business. Alternatively, as well as belonging to the parent institution with its attendant infrastructure, charity shops create their own internal network of staff, shoppers and donors. By dint of the extended social affiliations of these people as individuals, connectivity is established between a charity shop and the wider social networks of its locality. However, this is less likely to occur where charity shop managers have little interest in or need of the locality (e.g. where donated goods are collected and dispatched to shops centrally) and/or where charity shop work is the main public 'social' activity of volunteers.

Where dense social networks do occur through a charity shop, it can become a hub in its locality, providing a range of 'services' including social contact, recycling of used goods, consumption choice and social engagement through voluntary work as well as explicit services such as library facilities or acting as an (in)formal meeting point. Where reciprocation of services occurs between a charity shop and its locality in the form of community service labour, the charity shop can be argued to be part of the shadow state, an area populated by other voluntary organisations providing publicly funded services.

Lifestyle, life cycle and the charity shop

The concept of life cycle binds the experience of charity retailing and the charity shop sector, through the Wheel of Retailing, with individuals' experience of charity shops as donors, shoppers, volunteers and paid staff, each influenced in part by their stage of lifecycle. However, while a significant factor in the exchange of goods in charity shops, life cycle is overlain by lifestyle, economics, gender and a host of other factors.

The overwhelmingly dominant item purchased in charity shops is clothing, and this is perceived largely as a transaction between women: shoppers and shop staff. While this generalisation might have a strong basis, it represents a simple picture of what has been seen to be a complex sector within which complex social relations and consumption choices are made. As seen in Chapter 3, there are definite relationships between age, socio-economic class, gender and lifestyle choices influencing consumption in charity shops. Findings suggest an expected pattern, with those who are older and poorer being most likely to channel some of their consumption through charity shops, where they might expect to maximise the returns for their spending in a low-cost environment. However, there are further variations and complications of this simple pattern, including marked regional variations, with Scotland recording the lowest and the south of England the highest participation rates in charity shop consumption.

The main influences on purchasing motivation and consumption patterns are primarily the cheap prices (i.e. thrift) and the desire to support (the) charity. The attraction of unusual goods (especially period pieces and other collectables), proximity and convenience, and ethical positional consumption favouring fair trade or recycled goods also represent significant influences. Detailed analysis of these influences suggests that each of them relates to particular social groups. For example, those in the 18–30 age group of charity shoppers seek unusual goods, and all buy clothes, whereas those in the 31–40 age group were found to be the least likely to buy clothes (Maddrell 2001a). In contrast, 100 per cent of women in the same age group donate clothing to charity shops, suggesting circumstantial evidence to support the notion of speedy replacement consumption by this age group, with fashion-related over-consumption possibly being justified by donations of surplus clothing to charity shops. Fair trade goods also have their own tale to tell, being more widely purchased by women than by their male counterparts, the men being concentrated in the 18–30 age category (Maddrell 2001a), suggesting a political awareness and lifestyle choice adopted primarily by younger men, but also by women across the age groups. However, beyond these examples and in more general terms, age appeared to have a fairly minimal influence on purchasing patterns by type of goods.

Life cycle stage can be seen to affect donations to charity shops as well as consumption of goods. This might include goods associated with particular life stages, such as schooling, or life events such as birth, moving house and death, or more mundane tasks such as clearing out and decorating. Maternity and baby clothing would appear likely candidates for donation as these have a time limit on use, often long before an item is 'worn out'. However, these items (especially baby goods) appear only in limited quantities in charity shops for a number of reasons. These items do go on to second and subsequent cycles of consumption but primarily through private networks of kinship or resale such as local parent support groups (for example, the Lonsdale group (see Clarke 2000)) or car boot sales (Gregson and Crewe 1997), where they form a major offering. These private systems of exchange for children's clothing and equipment, whether by swapping or sale, allow the provenancing of goods (Clarke 2000), with hygiene and safety being particularly important factors influencing the purchase of second-hand goods for babies and small children. It also allows the recuperation of some costs by parents at what is often a life cycle period of financial constraint (due to reduced income and/or childcare costs) combined with ongoing expenditure.

The last years of a person's life are also a key period for donations of goods. Retirement, with a move to smaller accommodation or a care home, may motivate the relinquishing of material goods. Old age culminates in death and the disposal of the deceased's belongings (see also Curasi *et al.* 1998). These donations may go to the nearest charity shop or may be channelled by personal association with a given charity, for example if an individual has suffered from a disease or benefited from a local service. This can be seen in the case of independent charity shops raising funds for a local charity, notably hospice shops, whereby donations become part of the dialectical relationship between a patient and their family as both supporters and beneficiaries of the charity. The relationship can continue after the death of the patient, when their home is cleared, with goods being donated to the hospice shop, often in addition to formal bequests. As in the case of volunteering to help in charity shops (Maddrell 2000), these types of donations can be therapeutic and seen as a positive element of the grieving process. They can be seen not merely as a convenient but as a *constructive* disposal of the deceased's material goods, even as an opportunity to reinscribe the meaning of those goods from inalienable and therefore indisposable (because of the personal association) to alienable and disposable because the goods continue their 'social life' (Appadurai 1988) via an avenue approved by the deceased (see Chapter 4). In terms of general motivations for donating goods to charity shops, life cycle stage appears to have some bearing on attitudes to recycling, with one study (Maddrell 2001a) showing that recycling most influenced women between 31 and 40 years of age. This finding could suggest that environmental concern is most influential on women in the age group most associated in contemporary British society with child rearing.

If we look at the age profiles and motivations of volunteers in charity shops, it is possible to identify a correlation with life cycle stages and, to a lesser degree, lifestyle. Charity shop volunteers are predominantly made up of women over 55 years of age (Horne and Broadbridge 1994), and fewer than half of the volunteer respondents had a current/living partner (Maddrell 2000). These factors were reflected in the importance of the desire for company and something to do, suggesting the sociality of volunteer work in a shop setting. This heavy reliance of charity shops on retired volunteers is potentially threatened by the changing lifestyle ambitions of those moving into the Third Age group, who are seeking more than company and a sense of doing good in their retirement years (ibid.). However, this threat may yet prove to be unrealised, as an apparent decline of interest may be compensated for by the swelling of Third Age ranks by an ageing population coupled with a trend to early retirement.

Although dominated as a group by people of retirement age, charity shop volunteers are drawn from all age ranges, including young people motivated ideologically or for reasons of career development to work for charity and those compelled by government agencies in order to qualify for state benefits. School age and university student volunteers swell the 18–30 years category, reflecting the availability of time and/or involvement with various schemes and societies. This includes those fulfilling a requirement for community service on the Duke of Edinburgh Award scheme or through schools in the UK, or college fraternity or sorority requirements for community service in North America. Young volunteers at the beginning of their working life include students studying for business qualifications (such as

National Vocational Qualifications (NVQs)) or unemployed young people doing voluntary work in order to qualify for Job Seeker's Allowance under the Labour government's New Deal scheme. The use of probationers or licensed prisoners completing community service as part of a penal sentence has also added a younger (largely male) element to the volunteer workforce in both the UK and the USA (Maddrell 2000). The use of pre-parole licensed prisoners add a different dimension to observations on the links between life cycle and charity shops in the UK, as this volunteer work represents a privileged and often late stage in the life of their sentence (commonly prior to parole). Some prisoners went so far as to suggest that their volunteering represented an enhanced lifestyle and the possibility of a new stage in their life after release:

> 'It's getting me back into the community, getting used to working hours, I was just wasting my time inside.'
>
> (Licensed Prisoner 3, Oxford)

> 'I'm into it big time, the clothes be here. It's giving me inspiration for the rag trade from what I'm learning here, how to set it out, you know. I might like to open a little boutique. . . . The shop experience is what I've got most out of [community service].'
>
> (Licensed Prisoner 4, Oxford)

As Margaret Atwood's character Joan (in *Lady Oracle*, Virago) observes of second-hand possessions in Portobello Road, London, material goods experience different cycles of consumption within a product's life, these cycles being made possible by its alienable status, although this can be something that has to be negotiated or even achieved.

Within these lifecycles of material goods, items can be damaged and lose value, or gain patina and markers of authenticity, thereby increasing their value and desirability in the eyes of a particular consumer group. While the 'story' or provenance of a collectable item might increase its value (as in the case of an antique), for the majority of items sold in charity shops (and especially clothing), markers of their previous life or lives are deemed undesirable (see Gregson *et al.* 2000). Past histories are eradicated through a careful process of cleaning and re-presentation – consumers preferring to buy the illusion of sanitised goods, denying their past histories with their attendant threats of disease and death, or simply the presence of some Other. This is part of the attraction of the charity shop over the potentially more personal experience of consumption at the car boot sale. Whereas a parent may wish to be sure of the provenance of an item to be used by or for a small child (see Clarke 2000 and above), for the most part shoppers prefer to buy a second-hand item without confronting the person who now considers that same item undesirable. This preference can be reinforced in a local exchange where social embarrassment can occur over buying and reusing the Jones's curtains or the Ali's crockery – although, it has to be said that the same thing can occur with charity shop consumption where shops draw on a close network of donors and shoppers, as recounted between Mr Andrews and his daughter Polly in Mary McCarthy's *The Group*:

> 'through another of her charities, she [Aunt Julia] says, she picked up a rare Aubusson for a song.' Polly made a shocked noise. 'But where is it?' Mr. Andrews laughed. 'In her storeroom. She's waiting for its former owner to die. It might be embarrassing for Julia if the lady dropped in to call and found the rug underfoot.'
> (McCarthy 1954: 279)

As demonstrated here, consumption is not necessarily a passive or individualist undertaking, but can be active or shared (Sayer 2000). Although some consumers avoid charity shop goods because of a wider rejection of second-hand goods as incompatible with or a threat to their lifestyle, others positively choose the same items because their second-hand character displays their authenticity, as with 1970s retro clothing, original recordings of music, etc. These goods are often consumed as indicators or symbols of membership of a particular *bündes*, whether musical or relating to some other type of lifestyle sociation. Such consumption groups can be based on temporary fashion (for example, male fans of the Smiths in the 1980s would buy women's blouses from charity shops in emulation of the band's lead singer Morrissey) or represent more permanent lifestyle choices.

Lifestyle choices influenced by ideologies of environmental stewardship or sustainable development account for more permanent recurring consumption in charity and other alternative markets. Consumption based on these ethical positions has had a significant influence in generating demand for fair trade goods in charity shops, but this demand is potentially being undermined by the more widespread availability of fair trade food products in supermarkets. With the exception of these positional consumers, we might raise questions about the 'alternative' nature of consumption in charity shops. Is consumption in charity shops an opportunity to resist the discourses and power relations of mainstream retailing or, as Gregson suggests in the case of car boot sales (Gregson and Rose 2000), an opportunity to reinforce this discourse in their lives more cheaply? Such a rein-forcement can certainly be seen in the consumption of status labels or brands in charity shops, when consumers are literally buying into mainstream consumer values, albeit at a discounted price. Doing so may empower the economically disadvantaged consumer, and does cut across the prevailing mores of contemporary consumption based on rapid replacement consumption, replacing 'old' with *new* (more fashionable) goods, but it also reinforces existing mainstream societal values, which are increasingly brand focused (see Lury 1999). This sort of shopping in charity shops cannot be said to represent a true alter-native to mainstream consumption, which can probably be ascribed only to those who shop in charity shops on the basis of a chosen lifestyle, rather than by economic default.

The majority of charity shop consumers are influenced primarily in their consumption of second-hand goods by the attraction of thrift or 'experiencing shopping as saving', which Miller (1998) suggests is a near-universal imperative. However, while for some consumption is driven by the pleasure of perceived 'saving', a significant number of thrift-driven consumers in charity shops are making consumption choices based on limited economic agency, often due to life cycle stages, which may include being a student, unemployed, the parent of young children or a pensioner. Donors of second-hand goods for further consumption are drawn from these same groups, but also from those in stronger economic positions, including those financially empowered to lead a high-turnover, consumption lifestyle. Cohorts of volunteers are clearly drawn from distinct life cycle groups, primarily those of retired age but also those who have not yet started work and take on child-rearing responsibilities. For others, volunteering may facilit-ate a move to a new stage in their careers or life choices or life cycles, whether as a result of training, bereavement or release from prison. Current participation of individuals in charity shops, whether as con-sumers, donors or voluntary workers, clearly has strong links with lifecycle stages and commonly associated life events as well as lifestyle choices and constraints. Continuing to explore new, imaginative sources of volunteers and tailoring voluntary work to time offered, such as out-of-hours and episodic volunteering, despite potentially higher management costs, may well prove to be crucial to the con-tinued staffing of charity shops and the survival and success of the sector in the future.

Meeting social need or making a profit? The way forward for charity retailing

Charity shops emerged as a retailing phenomenon in the UK in the 1980s and 1990s, at a particular historical socio-economic/political juncture that saw widespread (but not universal) economic prosperity, a move to out-of-town shopping and a decline in community networks in many places. These changes included the decline, if not demise, of traditional forms of recycling such as local jumble sales, as well as an increased concern for the environment. They engendered a desire to recycle goods which had largely been lost during the years of post-war affluence. Car boot sales flourished in the same period as a means of private resale of goods for private profit, but charity shops offered a more altruistic and (significantly) anonymous form of disposal of goods, anonymity being favoured both by those unsure of the value of their cast-offs and those not wishing to be associated with the goods for a host of other reasons, as well as those simply being modest in their giving.

The exponential growth in the charity shop sector in the UK appears to have slowed, maybe even peaked, but unless value added tax (VAT) on second-hand goods is introduced (see Chapter 2), charity shops look set to stay on UK high streets. It is difficult to predict the future of a sector that has become so varied, as charity shops and individuals' expectations of them have become so complex and, arguably, contradictory. Given that the material and the social/cultural are mutually constituting, charity shop consumption is not simply a matter of an individual's lifestyle and taste, but the success of the charity shop in the future will depend on capturing the mood of society, and more specifically of consumers, and continuing to offer goods for which the use value is greater than the exchange value, in environments suitable to a varied customer base.

The charity shop sector, in line with other retail sectors, demonstrates an evolutionary and changing pattern, and here we explore the potential contradictions and conflicts inevitable as the sector develops. Issues discussed include charity retailers' policy and customer perceptions of customer service, and the provision of what is considered in many communities as a social service provided both to and by themselves.

At the heart of much of this debate is the issue of professionalisation. Conceptualisations of professionalisation within charity shops are varied but have been characterised to include the use of paid staff, the use of qualified 'professionals' and the adoption of hierarchical top-down management (Goodall 2000c). The large charity chains are increasingly becoming 'professionalised' in both their outlet presentation and their turnover targets. The more professionalised charity retailers have already taken on board standardised presentation in the form of corporate logos, bags, shop decor and window displays. There have also been a few examples of commercial advertising in newspapers and on posters, such as the television and cinema advertisement made by Leo Burnett for the launch of Oxfam's Origin collection of second-hand clothes in 1998, with its emphasis on retro fashion. Research findings suggest that further professionalism – especially in presentation – is an important element in attracting potential consumers resistant to the current charity shop offering (Maddrell 2001a). The main target groups are men of all ages and young people (male and female). Male non-patrons are looking for a wider range of more up-to-date merchandise that relates more clearly to their (aged and gendered) interests, notably fashionable (branded) clothes and sports goods (ibid.). Sourcing these goods through innovative approaches to collecting second-hand items and partnerships with producers of new goods (see below) is possible. However, these choices are not entirely straightforward, as staff and atmosphere are also significant factors at play in setting the ambience of the shop. Charity retailers will have to weigh the potential benefits of attracting a new clientele against any costs in terms of loss of existing customer base, as changes in offering and presentation are as likely to deter existing customers as attract new ones. Specialist shops and/or Internet marketing may well offer a solution in targeting particular consumer groups without alienating those loyal to the existing offering and shop type. Given that young people are commonly sensitive to ethical issues, it may be possible to target this consumption group. For example, large charity chains could consider creating a sub-chain of stores offering ethically produced (fair trade, recycled, etc.) fashionable new goods, or these could be marketed on the Internet.

The central question, which relates closely to the issue of professionalisation, is the primary one for all those seeking to enter into retailing – that is, 'What business are we in?' We have seen in the Introduction that the first charity shops were established as a provision for the poor, a place where they could enter the consumption arena, having been excluded through lack of financial means from other retail establishments. The first Oxfam shop, on the other hand, opened because of the potential to make money from donated goods in order to continue the good works of the charity. Most charities go into retailing in order to make money which will in turn enable them to carry out their individual, primary purpose such as the relief of poverty, the advancement of education or religion, or some other purpose perceived as beneficial to the community (*Charities Digest* 1995; also see Goodall 2000a). Here we have the beginning of a conflict of interest between direct social service (principally to the locality) and fund-raising through the use space of the charity shop. Many would argue that the two philosophies and shop functions are compatible, but as retail professionalisation increases, so costs rise and prices follow, potentially excluding those customers least able to pay.

While the overriding mission of the majority of contemporary charity shops is to make a profit, some charity shops continue in their aim to provide a service *in situ*, with those such as the Salvation Army having a commitment to an explicit localised social mission. Horne and Broadbridge (1995) have argued that temporary, low-cost (Category I) charity shops (see Chapter 2) are most likely to offer a service to those in economic need.

It is also important to note that to define the provision of a 'social service' in purely local terms would belittle the wider social benefits accruing from charity shop trading (without even considering the work achieved with funds raised). Clearly those shops that sell new goods produced by the beneficiaries of the charity (e.g. Mencap, a charity supporting mentally handicapped people) and those that sell fair trade goods from overseas collectives (again often sponsored by the agency, such as Oxfam initiatives) also provide a 'service', but one that can only be described on a national or even global scale of interrelationships. The question of the extent to which charity shops can be seen to relate to and specifically provide a service within the localities in which they are situated is an important and interesting one, and will be explored further below.

The Wheel of Retailing model discussed in Chapter 2, describes a progression from a basic, 'no frills' market entry phase to a trading up phase and finally a mature phase. It is easy to speculate that new charity shops will enter the market at the entry phase and either stay at that level, go forward to trade up and eventually reach maturation, or go out of business. If the shops reach maturity, the difficult question is what happens after this phase (see Figure 2.2). In order to overcome vulnerability at the mature phase, one way forward is for large charity retailers to form joint ventures with 'commercial retailers'. Joint ventures could also be formed between smaller charities in order for them to 'trade up' or to 'mature'. Both ventures hold potential pitfalls and need very careful consideration in terms of matching partners and relationship management before being undertaken.

One example of a partnership between two charities, one medical, the other concerned with childcare, came about because one of the charities had a great many volunteers willing to work in the shop and the other had solid financial and human resource management skills. By combining forces the joint venture flourished, with good management and a solid volunteer workforce. This pooling of resources can work very well at all phases of the retail cycle.

In the context of the reduced profit margins experienced by many charity retailers in 2000, additional expenditure on advertising and on the collecting and processing of donated goods threatens profits further. So the question to be asked is how can these aims be achieved without increasing overheads. While in the UK the charity shop sector is the main beneficiary of unwanted household goods (Horne and Hibbert 2001), there remains a shortfall in supply of goods for resale in the country's 6,000-plus charity shops. There are a number of possibilities for addressing this shortfall in donated goods. Strategies could include encouraging donations from young people (e.g. end-of-term/end-of-year campus collections at universities or collection points at young people's venues) and from locating small collection receptacles at places of sports activities (e.g. golf clubs) where men (and women) might find it easier to make donations. US armed forces bases commonly have a locally run thrift shop, often offering consignment sales as well as 100 per cent charity income sales; with a regular turnover of personnel, bases represent an ideal collection point for donated goods if security limitations can be worked around. This represents a policy of taking collection points of donated goods to target donors, as charities such as Humana and the Salvation Army are doing, with small-scale local collection banks often to be found near local shops or at local waste retrieval centres such as SCOPE book banks. These collection points are especially effective in locations without a nearby charity shop to compete for donations.

While mass advertising is beyond the economic possibilities of most charity retailers, the Internet revolution offers an opportunity to reach a wider audience of consumers and donors. Individual shops can advertise their location and stock (although advertising might be most effective in terms of a specialist/high-value discrete offering such as retro fashion or second-hand books). Alternatively, shops could collectively advertise their location to prospective consumers as is done on community pages on American town or newspaper Web sites. For example, in California there are area guides to second-hand shops (including thrift, resale, consignment and rummage shops), and the *Jupiter Courier* lists thrift shops for the Juno Beach area in its community information pages. These compilations of information are particularly effective in reaching, and attractive to, non-regular users or those visiting the area in pursuit of second-hand leisure shopping or bargain hunting. Alternatively, the Internet can be used to advertise charity shops to a given interest/support group, such as the United Jewish Appeal Federation of New York, which advertises its location and mission as follows: 'Shop for the best bargains around! Donate your gently used, fine-quality possessions! Our two thrift shops offer you an additional opportunity to help the community' (<http://www.thriftshopuja.org>, 24 April 2001).

Bought-in-new (BIN) goods are increasingly marketed by charities via Internet catalogues, allowing low-cost all-year advertising of merchandise to a relatively affluent and still male-dominated audience. The Save the Children Fund, for example (which operates in forty-two countries), has a number of nationally based online catalogues, including the USA Gift Collection. These virtual charity shops are being used to solicit donations and volunteers in the same way as physical shops and might be particularly effective in advertising vacancies for specialist volunteers and paid staff.

In addition to marketing BIN goods, charity retailers are also creating their own corporate auction sites for donated goods. These are used for the sale of collectables brought together centrally from donated stock – for example, Oxfam sells books (largely first editions and signed copies), music and stamps, etc. (Auction sites may also be effective in attracting donations of a similar type.) With organisation and imagination, the same system could be used to market other high-value collectables such as retro fashion, jewellery or porcelain, whether as an ongoing enterprise or as an annual event, with high-value goods separated out from local collections of donated goods and set aside for auction at national level. Other charities are able to maximise income from donated collectables by using commercial Internet auction sites, where although a sales premium might be accrued, the advantage of reaching a national or international group of consumers should ensure that the donated item is matched with the highest bidder. This method is particularly effective for small charities, as a single item can be marketed in this way. Clearly, alternative retailing, fund-raising and multiple cycles of consumption can be facilitated by the computer and communications revolution.

Not all goods donated to charities for conversion into profit through reselling are fit for resale (see Chapter 4). Sometimes this is due to a lack of thought by the donor (witness the donation of dirty or broken goods) and sometimes it is due to the specific request by a charity (such as those with a ban on underwear or the inability to safety-check electrical goods for resale). Alternative methods of conversion of these goods to profit, not sustainable for the second-hand market, are used through the medium of the charity shop. Ragging is the most widespread method; it means the selling of sub-standard textiles to rag merchants. This has been a lucrative exercise for many charities, with some using it as a revenue stream as an *alternative* to operating a conventional charity shop. However, during 1999–2000 competition from other countries caused rag prices to fall in the UK and many commercial rag merchants have closed, thus posing a real threat for the charity sector in terms of financial opportunity. It is estimated that the loss of ragging income has resulted in a drop by a quarter in the profits of UK housing charity Shelter, and has thus become a major concern for charity retailers (Phelan 1999a, b). An alternative method of selling on second-hand clothes is to sell them to non-industrialised countries – but this trade is banned by governments (such as that of Kenya) that are attempting to protect their indigenous clothing industries.

In the UK, discount stores constitute a competitive threat to charity shops, with outlets such as Matalan and Primark detracting from the appeal of charity shops as they are offering new goods at charity shop prices. This purchase of cheap short-life clothes might well have an effect on subsequent cycles of consumption, especially as these stores are attracting more affluent customers as well as those on limited incomes. Furthermore, if such clothes stores become more widespread, then the effect on the quality of donated goods in the future could be affected (see Goodall 2000c). We now see real competition from discount retailers that have filled the price gap between mainstream retailers and charity retailers, not least because discount stores have the advantage of being able to choose their own stock and can include sizes and style and colour ranges that satisfy customer wants.

Meanwhile, charity shops are struggling to recruit both voluntary labour and quality goods to sell. There is also a threat from high-quality retail outlets selling seconds or surplus from high street or designer shops, such as the Clarks Village in Street and Bicester Village in Oxfordshire. If a Karen Millen jacket or French Connection skirt can be bought for £10, there is direct competition for the business of the thrifty but label-conscious shopper, with charity shops offering used and less up-to-date quality clothing at similar prices. Sourcing surplus/seconds clothing goods might be an opportunity for charity shops to establish a new clothing niche, as suggested as a strategy by Mintel (1997), although they would be in competition for the supply of clothing with other existing 'seconds'/surplus retailers. An alternative would be for a given charity to establish a link with particular producers/retailers, as in the case of the Trendythreads thrift shop in Indianapolis, which receives slight seconds from the Liz Claiborne factory nearby. Given the orientation to brands and particularly 'designer' brands in contemporary consumption, any foot hold that charity retailers can achieve in this market would be likely to attract new and increased custom.

There is a constant debate amongst charity retailers as to the relative merits of BIN goods *vis-à-vis* second-hand goods. However, ultimately it is doubtful whether the majority of charity retailers would be willing to forgo the amenity of rate relief in order to sell more new goods, which might change the nature of the shop and its customers. There might also be an impact on donations: it could be that only better-quality goods would be offered (reducing sorting and disposal) or that goods would be disposed of to other charity outlets, for example *ad hoc* jumble sales, or sold at car boot sales and the like. Shop volunteers would also be affected by the move to sell a greater proportion of new goods, as many are in the business because they too enjoy the 'thrill' and excitement of selling donated goods which are an 'unknown quantity'. The selling of new goods would inevitably mean volunteers having to use more sophisticated technology and would limit negotiation of prices and the sense of autonomy (and hence power) that comes with pricing goods. If VAT were to be added to donated goods – it has been a threat to the sector for many users – the accounting structures would be more complicated and so the professional wheel would turn round a notch, and the 'thrift' rationale of the shops would inevitably fall to those individual shops coming in at the lower end of the market. The issue of further taxation is an ongoing threat to the operations of UK charity shops, but it is interesting to note that the majority of US states do not charge sales tax on donated goods. Where sales tax was imposed, it was subsequently repealed. For example, it was introduced in Nevada in 1992 but repealed in 1996.

Charity shops are engaged in negotiating the tensions between the processes of professionalisation and what are considered to be reasonable expectations of volunteers, through appropriate and/or selective training coupled with the employment of professional managers with retail experience. Within this evolving framework, volunteers are particularly able to meet the need for part-time specialist services, which includes offering professional training as well as mending and valuing high-value goods. Although the recent period of professionalisation in charity shops has seen the widespread introduction of paid managers, profit maximisation in the sector still relies significantly on unpaid labour in the form of volunteers. For some charity shops, community service workers have become a key source of volunteer hours, as have licensed prisoners, who will work a full five-day week, making them pivotal team members (Maddrell 2000). From a managerial point of view there are significant benefits to having a volunteer workforce, which can offer these blocks of time as well as personal attention and service to customers to a standard they may not experience in other comparable retail outlets.

For those charity shops and chains that prioritise fund-raising, a number of strategies are available to extend markets and turnover. Some shops will find their future in niche marketing, whether in terms of a niche specialist offering (such as furniture or reconditioned computers) or a wider offering to a small niche of society, perhaps spatially or socially demarcated. A growth in BIN goods has been predicted (Mintel 1997). This may serve to attract shoppers previously resistant to charity shops limited to selling second-hand goods (particularly in the case of shops selling nothing but BIN goods), but has resulted in mixed responses within existing 'mixed' charity shops. BIN shops may also find themselves increasingly redundant in forthcoming years in the face of Internet sales of new goods. It may be appropriate for some charity traders to sidestep the issue of in-shop BIN goods, with associated complexities of taxation status, etc., by moving directly into Internet marketing as that sector itself takes root and grows. Internet marketing has the advantage of relatively low overheads and access to a previously inaccessible customer base, potentially a different sort of lifestyle and interest group, looking for different sorts of goods. Internet sales are bound to grow for both new goods and high-value donated collectables – but there will be a need for differentiation in virtual charity shops, as in physical charity shops and catalogues, the latter having become increasingly homogenised in recent years. Other charities, reflecting their wider mission, may continue in retailing, but primarily as a means of outreach and provision of 'social service' such as job creation, training provision and reinforcement of social networks, with profits becoming of secondary importance. These shops may seek to become more embedded in local networks, to become adopted as a local cause, even if originally 'planted' by a marketing decision rather than having grown 'organically' out of a local initiative.

Despite differences in national discourses of consumption, some charities have succeeded in internationalising their operations. Examples include the Save the Children Fund, with its universal mission, or Goodwill, which is using its US model in Russia, initially supplied with US-donated goods. Such internationalisation can be seen as part of an increasing trend on the part of charity retailers to diversify in order to maximise both fund-raising and wider social aims. This trend can be seen in the UK in the case of Oxfam, with its well-established infrastructure of fair trade suppliers, shops, warehouses, catalogues, Internet auctions and gift sales. Such diversification can be effective on both large and small scales, as seen in the case of Alpha Ministries Inc. in Australia, which has succeeded in combining three second-hand clothing 'opp' shops, a small factory processing rags for cleaning cloths for industrial or domestic use and offering 20- or 40-foot containers of quality second-hand clothing for export. Funds raised support its work locally in Australia with family, drug and alcohol counselling, profits from the sale of goods overseas funding domestic charitable work, the converse of the likes of Oxfam, which raise money to support projects abroad. Another church-based charity, St Vincent de Paul, which is an international Catholic charitable organisation, runs charity shops in Ireland, Australia, the USA and Canada. In Ottawa in Canada, St Vincent de Paul combines two charity shops and channelling the donation of goods directly to the local needy. Non-store-quality goods are baled and sent to non-industrialised countries, and the remainder are washed and sterilised for wiper rag manufacturing. In order to support this programme a number of collection systems are used, including textile banks, collection programmes, local clothing drives and advertising on the Internet for general and specific requests such as the need for school uniforms at the beginning of the school year. Once more the use of the Internet allows a sophisticated matching of supply to demand for seasonal or other needs, as well as the promotion of the charity's work, including the environmental externalities of this recycling: 'Every pound of textiles diverted to Vincent de Paul extends the life of the . . . landfill while supporting a good cause' (<http://svdp.ottawa.com/ragshop>, 21 April 2001). In New York, Housing Works, a charity providing housing, support services and advocacy for the homeless with Aids or HIV infection, runs three thrift shops and the Used Book café, promoting its locales as desirable places to be: 'Shop chic, save seriously' (<http://www.housingworks.baweb.com>).

These examples illustrate the continued applicability of the Salvation Army's 1908 description of 'waste turned to good account' (*The War Cry*, 8 February 1908), as well as the complex operations undertaken and systems used by charities to raise funds in and through their charity shops and associated trading endeavours, in which they often see themselves as multifunctional and multi-mission. The most effective of these either seem to be deeply embedded in the support network of a locality or a specific interest group, or alternatively run a complex servicing infrastructure supplying shops with donated goods collected and processed centrally. However, as some charities demonstrate, the two approaches do not have to be mutually exclusive.

The charity shop sector has had significant success in normalising second-hand consumption, but will at best have limited success and at worst stagnate or decline if it continues to homogenise its offering and appeal to the same target groups. Indeed, in 2000–1 three charities in the UK ceased their trading altogether (World Vision, National Relate and the National Society for the Prevention of Cruelty to Children) (Goodall 2000b). Exploring the merits of creating or appealing to what Mort (1996) describes as 'different topographies of taste' of different lifestyle groups and combining these with the most appropriate form of marketing, whether traditional shop, e-commerce or specialist outlet, is a means of reaching chosen target groups. Charity shops are as much a social as a retailing phenomenon and need to be seen as such if we are to understand both their commercial success and social impact.

Bibliography

Ali, M. (1996) *The DIY Guide to Marketing for Charity and Voluntary Organisations*, Directory of Social Change, London.

Appadurai, A. (ed.) (1986) *The Social Life of Things*, Cambridge University Press, Cambridge.

Atwood, M. (1982) *Lady Oracle*, Virago, London.

Bartlett, J. (1990) 'On the crest of an ethical retail wave', *Accountancy*, December, 68–70.

Benaday, D. (1997) 'Charity shops adapt to survive', *Marketing Week*, 19 June.

Berman, B. and Evans, J. R. (1995) *Retail Management: A Strategic Approach*, Prentice Hall International Editions, Englewood Cliffs, NJ.

Blois, K. J. (1987) 'Marketing for non-profit organizations', in M. J. Baker (ed.) *The Marketing Book*, Heinemann, London.

Blomley, N. (1996) ' "I'd like to dress her all over": masculinity, power and retail space', in N. Wrigley and M. Lowe (eds) *Retailing, Consumption and Capital: Towards the New Retail Geography*, Longman, London.

Booth, W. (1890) *In Darkest England and the Way Out*, Charles Knight, London.

Broadbridge, A. and Horne, S. (1996) 'Volunteers in charity retailing: recruitment and training', *Nonprofit Management and Leadership* 6: 255–70.

Brooks, N. (1996) 'UK trading: a guide to charities and the tax implications', *Journal of Nonprofit and Voluntary Sector Marketing* 1(3): 219–24.

Brown, S. (1987) 'The Wheel of Retailing', *International Journal of Retailing* 3(1): 16–37.

Brown, S. (1990) 'The Wheel of Retailing past and future', *Journal of Retailing* 66(2): 143–9.

Brown, S. (1992) 'The wheel of retail gravitation?', *Environment and Planning A* 24: 1409–39.

Brown Barrat, M. (1993) *Fair Trade: Reform and Realities in the International Trading System*, Zed Books, London.

Bruce, I. (1998) *Successful Charity Marketing: Meeting Need*, 2nd edition, ICSA Publishing with Prentice Hall Europe, Hemel Hempstead, UK.

Bucklin, L. (1972) *Competition and Evolution in the Distributive Trades*, Prentice Hall, Englewood Cliffs, NJ.

Campbell, C. (1986) *The Romantic Ethic and the Spirit of Modern Consumerism*, Blackwell, Oxford.

Charities Digest (1995) 101st edition, Family Welfare Association, London.

Chattoe, E. (2000) 'Charity shops as second-hand markets', *International Journal of Nonprofit and Voluntary Sector Marketing* 5: 153–60.

Chisnall, Peter M. (1992) *Marketing Research*, McGraw-Hill, Maidenhead, UK.

Clammer, J. (1992) 'Aesthetics of the self: shopping and social being in contemporary urban Japan', in R. Shields (ed.) *Lifestyle Shopping: The Subject of Consumption*, Routledge, London.

Clarke, A. (2000) ' "Mother swapping": the trafficking of nearly new children's wear', in P. A. Jackson, M. Lowe, D. Miller and F. Mort (eds) *Commercial Cultures: Economies, Practices, Spaces*, Berg, Oxford.

Clarke, A. (1998) 'Window shopping at home: classifieds, catalogues and new consumer skills', in D. Miller (ed.) *Material Cultures: Why Some Things Matter*, UCL Press, London.

Cohen, J. (1995) 'An examination of a customer profile: a study of Oxfam's customers in Stirling', unpublished final year dissertation, University of Stirling.

Corporate Intelligence (1992) *Charity Shops in the UK*, Corporate Intelligence Research Publications, London.

Cox, R. and Brittain, P. (1988) *Retail Management*, Pitman, London.

Crewe, L. and Gregson, N. (1998) 'Tales of the unexpected: exploring car boot sales as marginal spaces of contemporary consumption', *Transactions of the Institute of British Geographers* NS 23: 39–53.

Crewe, L. and Lowe, M. (1996) 'United colours: globalization and localization tendencies in fashion retailing', in N. Wrigley and M. Lowe (eds) *Retailing, Consumption and Capital: Towards the New Retail Geography*, Jossey-Bass, San Francisco.

Curasi, C. F., Price, L. L. and Arnould, E. J. (1998) 'A meaning transfer model of the disposition decisions of older consumers', *European Advances in Consumer Research* 3: 211–21.

Dalrymple, D. J. and Parsons, L. J. (1995) *Marketing Management: Texts and Cases*, 6th edition, John Wiley, New York.

D'Amico, M. (1983) 'Discussants' comments', in J. L. Summey *et al.* (eds) *Marketing Theories and Concepts for an Era of Change*, Southern Marketing Association, Carbondale, Ill.

Davis Smith, L. (2000) 'Volunteering and social development', *Voluntary Action* 3: 9–23.

Dees, J. G. (1998) 'Enterprising nonprofits', *Harvard Business Review,* January/February, 55–67.

Dibb, S., Simkin, L., Pride, W. and Ferrell, O. (1994) *Marketing: Concepts and Strategies*, Houghton Mifflin, Boston.

Dickens, P. (1990) *Urban Sociology: Society, Locality and Human Nature*, Harvester Wheatsheaf, London.

Dittmar, H. (1992) *The Social Psychology of Material Possessions: To Have Is to Be*, Harvester Wheatsheaf, Hemel Hempstead.

Domosh, M. (1996) 'The feminized retail landscape: gender, ideology and consumption culture in nineteenth century New York City', in N. Wrigley and M. Lowe (eds) *Retailing, Consumption and Capital: Towards a New Retail Geography*, Longman, Harlow, UK.

Doyle, P. (1991) 'Managing the marketing mix', in M. J. Baker (ed.) *The Marketing Book*, 2nd edition, Heinemann, London.

Eaglesham, J. (1996) 'Charity shops and the cash that won't reach the needy', *The Independent on Sunday*, 2 February.

Ellis, J. (1996) 'Charity shops: friend or foe?', BA dissertation, University of Stirling, unpublished.

European Fair Trade Association (1995) *Fair Trade Yearbook*, Druck in De Veer, Ghent.

Fair Trade Foundation, <www.fairtrade.co.uk>.

Fair Trade Issue (2000) 'Fair or free trade: the facts', *New Internationalist*, April.

Foster, J. (1997) 'Volunteering by members of black and minority ethnic communities in Britain', in C. Pharoah (ed.) *Dimensions of the Voluntary Sector*, Charities Aid Foundation, West Malling, UK.

Foster, V. (1997) 'What value should be placed on volunteering?', in C. Pharoah (ed.) *Dimensions of the Voluntary Sector*, Charities Aid Foundation, West Malling, UK.

Foxall, G. and Goldsmith, R. (1994) *Consumer Psychology for Marketing*, Routledge, London.

Freathy, P. (1997) 'Employment theory and the Wheel of Retailing: segmenting the circle', *Services Industries Journal* 17(3): 413–31.

Gabor, A. (1977) *Pricing: Principles and Practices*, Heinemann, London.

Gaskin, C. (1997) 'Assessing the economic value and cost of volunteers', in C. Pharoah (ed.) *Dimensions of the Voluntary Sector*, Charities Aid Foundation, London.

Gipsrud, G. (1986) 'Market structure, perceived competition and expected competitor reactions in retailing', *Research in Marketing* 8: 251–71.

Golden, L. and Zimmerman, D. (1986) *Effective Retailing*, Houghton Mifflin, Boston.

Gondouin, S. (1997) 'Religion and buyer behaviour: do religious customers have a specific behaviour?', BA dissertation, University of Stirling, unpublished.

Goodall, R. (2000a) 'Charity shops in sector context: the view from the boardroom', *International Journal of Nonprofit and Voluntary Sector Marketing* 5(2): 105–12.

Goodall, R. (2000b) 'Slipping away: charity shops feel the high-street pinch', *NGO Finance* 6: 20–36.

Goodall, R. (2000c) 'Organising cultures: voluntarism and professionalisation in the UK charity shops', *Voluntary Action* 3(1): 43–57.

Goss, K. (1999) 'Volunteering and the long civic generation', *Nonprofit and Voluntary Sector Quarterly* 28: 378–415.

Gregson, N. and Crewe, L. (1997a) 'The bargain, the knowledge, and the spectacle: making sense of consumption in the space of the car-boot sale', *Environment and Planning D: Society and Space* 15: 87–112.

Gregson, N. and Crewe, L. (1997b) 'Performance and possession: rethinking the act of purchase in the light of the car boot sale', *Journal of Material Culture* 2(2): 241–63.

Gregson, N. and Crewe, L. (1998) 'Dusting down second-hand Rose: gendered identities and the world of second-hand goods in the space of the car boot sale', *Gender, Place and Culture* 5: 77–100.

Gregson, N. and Rose, G. (2000) 'Taking Butler elsewhere: performativities, spatialities and subjectivities', *Environment and Planning D: Society and Space* 18: 433–52.

Gregson, N., Brooks, K. and Crewe, L. (2000) 'Narratives of consumption and the body in the space of the charity shop', in P. Jackson, M. Lowe, D. Miller and F. Mort (eds) *Commercial Cultures: Economies, Practices, Spaces*, Berg, Oxford.

Grobman, G. M. (2000) 'E-shopping for charity: where do you fit in?', *International Journal of Nonprofit and Voluntary Sector Marketing* 5: 174–8.

Guy, B. S. and Patton, W. E. (1989) 'The marketing of altruistic causes: understanding why people help', *Journal of Consumer Marketing* 6(1): 19–30.

Hanna, N. and Dodge, H. R. (1995) *Pricing Policies and Procedures*, Macmillan, Basingstoke, UK.

Hannagan, T. J. (1992) *Marketing for the Nonprofit Sector*, Macmillan, Basingstoke, UK.

Harper, D. V. (1966) *Price Policy and Procedure*, Harcourt, Brace and World, New York.

Hermann, S. (1989) *Price Management*, Elsevier Science Publishers, Amsterdam.

Herrmann, J. and Soiffer, S. M. (1984) 'For fun and profit: an analysis of the American garage sale', *Urban Life* 12: 397–421.

Hetherington, K. (1992) 'Stonehenge and its festival: spaces of consumption', in R. Shields (ed.) *Lifestyle Shopping: The Subject of Consumption*, Routledge, London.

'High street charity' (1992) *Choice*, September, p. 51.

Holden, C. (1996) 'Retail outlets as a successful fundraising medium', *Journal of Nonprofit and Voluntary Sector Marketing* 1(3): 213–18.

Hollander, S. C. (1960) 'The Wheel of Retailing', *Journal of Marketing* 21(1): 37–42.

Horne, S. and Hibbert, S. (2001) 'What to do with the unwanted: how consumers dispose of used goods', *Proceedings of the 30th European Marketing Academy Conference*, May, Bergen.

Horne, S. (1995) 'L'attività commerciale nelle organizzazioni non profit e il sistema impositivo: il realizzarsi della concorrenza', *Nonprofit: Diritto & Management degli Enti Non Commerciali* 1: 609–17.

Horne, S. (1998) 'Charity shops in the UK', *International Journal of Retail and Distribution Management* 26(4–5): 155–61.

Horne, S. (2000) 'The charity shop: purpose and change', *International Journal of Nonprofit and Voluntary Sector Marketing* 5(2): 113–24.

Horne, S. and Broadbridge, A. (1993) 'From Rags to Riches: A Classification of Charity Shops', *Working Paper 9302*, Institute for Retail Studies, Stirling University.

Horne, S. and Broadbridge, A. (1994) 'The charity shop volunteer in Scotland: greatest asset or biggest headache?', *Voluntas* 5: 205–18.

Horne, S. and Broadbridge, A. (1995) 'Charity shops: a classification by merchandise mix', *International Journal of Retail and Distribution Management* 23(7): 17–23.

Horne, S. and Maddrell, A. (2000) Editorial, *International Journal of Nonprofit and Voluntary Sector Marketing* 5(2): 101–2.

Howe, W. S. (1992) *Retailing Management*, Macmillan, London.

Huat Chua, B. (1992) 'Shopping for women's fashion in Singapore', in R. Shields (ed.) *Lifestyle Shopping: The Subject of Consumption*, Routledge, London.

Ilsley, P. J. (1990) *Enhancing the Volunteer Experience: New Insights on Strengthening Volunteer Participation, Learning and Commitment*, Jossey-Bass, San Francisco.

Jackson, P. and Thrift, N. (1995) 'Geographies of consumption', in D. Miller (ed.) *Acknowledging Consumption: A Review of New Studies*, Routledge, London.

Jackson, P., Lowe, M., Miller, D. and Mort, F. (eds) *Commercial Cultures: Economies, Practices, Spaces*, Berg, Oxford.

James, D., Walker, B. and Etzel, M. J. (1981) *Retailing Today*, Harcourt Brace Jovanovich, New York.

Jarvis, C. and Hancock, R. (1997) 'Trends in volunteering and the implications for the future', in C. Pharoah (ed.) *Dimensions of the Voluntary Sector*, Charities Aid Foundation, London.

Keating, M. (1998) 'Faith, hope and tax relief', *Guardian*, 15 December.

Kent, R. A. (1993) *Marketing Research in Action*, Routledge, London.

Kenwright, H. (2000) 'Volunteering to learn: approaches to educational provision for volunteers and their clients', *Voluntary Action* 3: 59–72.

Kopytoff, I. (1986) 'The cultural biography of things: commoditization as process', in A. Appadurai (ed.) *The Social Life of Things*, Cambridge University Press, Cambridge.

Kotler, P. and Andreasen. A. R. (1991) *Strategic Marketing for Nonprofit Organizations*, 4th edition, Englewood Cliffs, NJ: Prentice Hall.

Lord, K. and Putrevu, S. (1998) 'Acceptance of recycling appeals: the moderating role of perceived consumer effectiveness', *Journal of Marketing Management*, 14(6): 581–91.

Lovelock, C. H. and Weinberg, C. B. (1983) 'Retailing strategies for public and non-profit organisations', *Journal of Retailing* 59(3): 93–115.

Lowe, M. and Wrigley, N. (1996) 'Towards the new retail geography', in N. Wrigley and M. Lowe (eds) *Retailing, Consumption and Capital*, Longman, Harlow, UK.

Lukka, P. and Locke, M. (2000) 'Faith, voluntary action and social policy: a review of research', *Voluntary Action* 3: 25–41.

Lunt, P. and Livingstone, S. (1992) *Mass Consumption and Personal Identity: Everyday Economic Experience*, Open University Press, Buckingham and Bristol.

Lury, C. (1999) *Consumer Culture*, Polity, Cambridge.

Lynn, R. and Davis Smith, I. (1991) 'The 1991 National Survey of Voluntary Activity in the UK', second series, paper no. 1, *Voluntary Action Research*, Volunteer Centre, Berkhamstead, UK.

McCarthy, M. (1954) *The Group*, Penguin, London.

McCarty, J. A. and Shrum, L. J. (1993) 'A structural equation analysis of the relationship of personal values, attitudes and beliefs about recycling and the recycling of solid waste products', *Advances in Consumer Research* 20: 641–6.

McClelland, D. C. (1961) *The Achieving Society*, Van Nostrand, Princeton, NJ.

McCracken, G. (1988) *Culture and Consumption: New Approaches to the Symbolic Character of Consumer Goods and Activities*, Indiana University Press, Bloomington and Indianopolis.

McCracken, G. (1990) *Culture and Consumption: New Approaches to the Symbolic Character of Consumer Goods and Activities*, 2nd edition, Indiana University Press, Bloomington and Indianapolis.

McDowell, L. (1996) *Capital Culture: Gender at Work in the City*, Blackwell, Oxford.

McGoldrick, P. J. (1990) *Retail Marketing*, McGraw-Hill, London.

McLoone, P. (1994) *Carstairs Scores for Scottish Postcode Sectors from the 1991 Census*, Public Health Research Unit, University of Glasgow.

McNair, M. and May, E. (1978) 'The next revolution of the retailing wheel', *Harvard Business Review* 56(5): 89–91.

McNair, M. P. (1958) 'Significant trends and developments in the post-war period', in A. B. Smith (ed.) *Competitive Distribution in a Free High Level Economy and Its Implications for the University*, University of Pittsburgh Press, Pittsburgh.

McQuillan, J. (ed.) (1988) *Charity Trends*, 11th edition, Charities Aid Foundation, Tonbridge, UK.

Maddrell, A. (1999) 'Charity shops: community service? Charity shops, retailing, consumption and society', unpublished conference paper, Charity Shops Conference, Westminster College, Oxford, April.

Maddrell, A. (2000) ' "You just can't get the staff these days": the challenges and opportunties of working with volunteers in the charity shop – an Oxford case study', *Journal of Nonprofit and Voluntary Sector Marketing* 2(5): 125–40.

Maddrell, A. (2001a) 'Charity shops in Oxford: a report to participating shops', Unpublished.

Maddrell, A. (2001b) 'Charity shops in the Isle of Man: a report to participating shops', Unpublished.

Max Havelaar Stichting, <www.maxhavelaar.nl>, Amsterdam.

Miller, D. (ed.) *Acknowledging Consumption*, Routledge, London.

Miller, D. (1995b) 'Consumption as the vanguard of history', in D. Miller (ed.) *Acknowledging Consumption*, Routledge, London.

Miller, D. (1998) *A Theory of Shopping*, Polity, Cambridge.

Miller, D. (2000) 'The birth of value', in P. Jackson, M. Lowe, D. Miller and F. Mort (eds) *Commercial Cultures: Economies, Practices, Spaces*, Berg, Oxford.

Milligan, C. (2000) ' "Breaking the asylum": developments in the geography of mental ill-health – the influence of the informal sector', *Health and Place* 6: 189–200.

Milofsky, C. (ed.) (1988a) *Community Organizations: Studies in Resource Mobilization and Exchange*, Oxford University Press, Oxford.

Milofsky, C. (1988b) 'Scarcity and Community', in C. Milofsky (ed.) *Community Organizations: Studies in Resource Mobilization and Exchange*, Oxford University Press, Oxford.

Milofsky, C. (1988c) 'Structure and process in community self-help organizations', in C. Milofsky (ed.) *Community Organizations: Studies in Resource Mobilization and Exchange*, Oxford University Press, Oxford.

Mintel (1997) 'Charity shop retailing', *Mintel Retail Intelligence*, June, London.

Monroe, K. B. (1979) *Pricing: Making Profitable Decisions*, McGraw-Hill, London.

Mort, F. (1996) *Culture of Consumption: Masculinities and Social Space in Late Twentieth-Century Britain*, Routledge, London.

Nixon, S. (1992) 'Have you got the look? Masculinities and shopping spectacle', in R. Shields (ed.) *Lifestyle Shopping: The Subject of Consumption*, Routledge, London.

Octon, C. M. (1983) 'A re-examination of marketing for British non-profit organizations', *European Journal of Marketing* 17(5): 40–1.

Oliver, R. L. (1997) *Satisfaction: A Behavioral Perspective on the Consumer*, McGraw-Hill, New York.

Paddison, A. (2000) 'Charity shops on the high street: complementary or unwanted neighbour?', *Journal of Nonprofit and Voluntary Sector Marketing* 5(2): 161–72.

Parsons, L. (1996) 'Introducing charity shopping to contemporary debates on consumption', unpublished M.Sc. thesis, University of Bristol.

Parsons, L. (2000) 'New goods, old records and second-hand suits', *Journal of Nonprofit and Voluntary Sector Marketing* 5(2): 141–52.

Phelan, D. (1994) 'Charity shops reach saturation point: diminishing returns set in', *NGO Finance* 4(3): 12–22.

Phelan, D. (1996) 'High street wars hot up: charity shops face rates offensive', *NGO Finance* 6(3): 18–28.

Phelan, P. (1997) 'Coming of age in the high street: a brighter future for charity shops?', *NGO Finance* 7: 18–26.

Phelan, D. (1999a) 'Working on the chain gang: hard labour for charity shops', *NGO Finance* 9(6): 16–29.

Phelan, D. (1999b) 'The 1999 charity shops survey', *NGO Finance* 9(6): 16–29.

Phelan, D., Lamont, H. and Howley, P. (1998) 'Charity shops sailing fair – but storm clouds blot retail horizon', *NGO Finance* 8(5): 3–13.

Poovey, M. (1988) *Uneven Development: The Ideological Work of Gender in Mid-Victorian England*, University of Chicago Press, Chicago.

Rausing, S. (1998) 'Signs of the new nation: gift exchange, consumption and aid on a former collective farm in north-west Estonia', in D. Miller (ed.) *Material Cultures: Why Some Things Matter*, UCL Press, London.

St Leger, M. (1993) 'Shops operated by the top 400 charities', in S. K. E. Saxon-Harrold (ed.) *Researching the Voluntary Sector*, Charities Action Fund, West Malling, UK.

Sandall, R. (1955) *The History of the Salvation Army*, Vol. 3, Thomas Nelson, London.

Sarfit, R. D. and Merrill, L. S. W. (2000) 'Management implications of contemporary trends in voluntarism in the United States and Canada', *Voluntary Action* 3: 73–88.

Savitt, R. (1988) 'Comment: "The Wheel of Retailing" ', *International Journal of Retailing* 3(1): 38–40.

Sayer, A. (2000) 'Critical and uncritical cultural turns', in I. Cook, D. Crouch, S. Naylor and J. R. Ryan (eds) *Cultural Turns/Geographical Turns*, Prentice Hall, London.

'Sell harder sweet charity' (1998) *Marketing*, 14 May: 14.

Sherry, J. F. Jr (1983) 'A socio-cultural analysis of a Midwestern flea market', *Journal of Consumer Research*, 17: 13–30.

Shields, R. (1992) 'The individual, consumption cultures and the fate of the community', in R. Shields (ed.) *Lifestyle Shopping: The Subject of Consumption*, Routledge, London.

Simon, H. (1989) *Price Management*, Elsevier Science Publishers, Amsterdam.

Simon, B., Sturmer, S. and Steffens, K. (2000) 'Helping individuals or group members? The role of individuals and collective identification in AIDS volunteerism', *Personality and Social Psychology Bulletin* 26: 497–506.

Slater, D. (2000) 'Consumption without scarcity: exchange and normativity in an internet setting', in P. Jackson, M. Lowe, D. Miller and F. Mort (eds) *Commercial Cultures: Economies, Practices, Spaces*, Berg, Oxford.

Slingsby, E. (1997) 'An examination of pricing in charity shops', unpublished dissertation, Department of Marketing, University of Stirling.

Stone, J., Horne, S. and Hibbert, S. A. (1996) 'Car boot sales: a study of shopping motives in an alternative retail format', *International Journal of Retail and Distribution Management* 24(11): 4–15.

Stroeker, N. E. and Antonides, G. (1997) 'The process of reaching an agreement in second-hand markets for consumer durables', *Journal of Economic Psychology* 18(4): 341–67.

Strong, C. (1996) 'Features contributing to the growth of ethical consumerism: a preliminary investigation', *Marketing Intelligence and Planning* 14(5): 5–13.

Sue Ryder (1992) *High Street Charity*, Sue Ryder, London.

Tönnies, F. (1887) *Gemeinschaft und Gesellschaft*. Translated by C. P. Loomis (1955) as *Community and Association*, Routledge & Kegan Paul, London.

van der Veen, V. (2000) 'On complex communication: the case of fair trade', M.Sc. dissertation, University of Stirling, unpublished.

Whitfield, D. and Scott, D. (1993) *Paying Back: Twenty Years of Community Service*, Waterside Press, Winchester.

Whithear, R. (1999) 'Charity shop volunteers: a case for tender loving care', Paper given at the Charity Shops, Retailing, Consumption and Society Conference, Westminster College, Oxford, April.

Wikstrom, S. R. (1997) 'The Changing Consumer in Sweden', *International Journal of Research in Marketing* 14(3): 261–74.

Williams, C. C. and Windebank, J. (2000) 'Modes of goods acquisition in deprived neighborhoods', *International Review of Retail, Distribution and Consumer Research*, 10(1): 73–94.

Winkler, J. (1983) *Pricing for Results*, Butterworth-Heinemann, Oxford.

Wrigley, N. and Lowe, M. (eds) *Retailing, Consumption and Capital*, Longman, Harlow, UK.

Young, M. M. (1991) 'Disposition of possessions during role transitions', *Advances in Consumer Research* 18: 33–9.

Index

152   *Index*

Volunteer Investment and Value
  Audit (VIVA) 74–5
volunteers 5, 7, 12, 15, 19, 31, 33,
  34, 36, 46, 71–96, 97, 98, 99, 119,
  120, 134; characteristics 73–84;
  contribution 84–8; and donations
  58, 61, 66, 68, 69, 85, 133; and
  life cycle 123–4, 126; motivation
  72, 78–81, 86, 123–4; number
  and importance 71–3; and pricing
  110–11, 117; recruitment 7, 28,
  82–4, 87, 89–96, 120, 126, 131,
  132; specialist 49, 50, 62, 77, 99,
  131, 133; time given 76, 81–2;
  training 83, 87–8, 90, 96, 99,
  133; value 74–7

warehouses 3, 57, 58, 59–70
Weinberg, C. B. 29
Wheel of Retailing 29, 30–3, 103,
  121, 129; staff and cyclical
  change 33–7
Whithear, R. 34, 77, 79, 80, 82, 83,
  86, 87, 97, 98
Wildfowl and Wetland Trust
  (WWT) 54
Winkler, J. 104, 109
World Vision 136
Wrigley, N. 11

Young, M. M. 62

Zimmerman, D. 106